Christianity in Crisis

NEW HOPE

REV. SUN MYUNG MOON

Holy Spirit Association for the Unification of World Christianity

Published by Vertizon, Inc., New York
Photos: Front cover by Don Landwehrle, The Image Bank
        Back cover by Robert R. Davis, New Future Photo

Printed in the United States of America
ISBN 0-910-62151-9

Contents

Foreword

Reverend Sun Myung Moon has now carried on his ministry in the United States for over a decade and a half. It was in 1971 that, responding to the call of God, he left his native Korea and journeyed to America. God had entrusted Reverend Moon to proclaim an essential, prophetic message to the American people, and especially to its Christian leaders, concerning America's responsibility in the world and the future challenges facing Christian churches. Although Reverend Moon could not speak English and was faced with an unfamiliar culture, he did not hesitate to speak out. Like the prophet Amos, who travelled from his native Judah to confront the leaders of the Northern Kingdom, Reverend Moon travelled throughout America speaking the truth which God is now revealing to people of the 20th century.

Reverend Moon carried his first "Day of Hope" tour to seven American cities in 1972. His second speaking tour of twenty-one American cities began on October 1, 1973 at Carnegie Hall in New York City. In each city he spoke on three consecutive evenings on the topic "Christianity in Crisis: New Hope." In city after city, large crowds listened with rapt attention to the message of God conveyed by the Reverend Moon. The excellent response encouraged him to extend his speaking tour to thirty-two additional cities, so that by the middle of 1974 he had presented his message in every state of the United States and in every major city. One speech from each evening in the series was published in the first edition of *Christianity in Crisis: New Hope* in 1974.

This new edition of *Christianity in Crisis: New Hope* also includes the two speeches which Reverend Moon gave in his third Day of Hope tour of eight cities at the end of 1974. His third opened on September 18, 1974 before a standing-room-only crowd of 25,000 at New York's Madison Square Garden. While he delivered his message, "The New Future of Christianity," an estimated 15,000 more gathered outside the Garden, trying to get a glimpse of this modern-day prophet. On the previous night, more than 1,700 distinguished guests gathered for a banquet at the Waldorf Astoria, where they heard Reverend Moon speak. Present were representatives of every segment of New York's citizenry — government officials, businessmen, educators, artists, religious leaders, diplomats, and the press—who listened spellbound to Reverend Moon's message, one quite different from the usual sermon delivered from a pulpit. These latter two speeches were first published in 1974 as *The New Future of Christianity*.

Why, after over a decade has passed, should these speeches be republished?

Reverend Moon is a prophet, not just an ordinary preacher or evangelist. Evangelists arise in every generation to inspire people to understand God and to follow Christ by expounding the message of Scripture. A prophet, on the other hand, is a revealer, a channel between God and humanity. God summons prophets only at those special moments when He wishes to reveal a specific message regarding His Will and His expectation for the people. Prophets arise in time of crisis, when God's people must be made aware of their responsibility in the face of impending danger. The words of the prophet carry with them a divine urgency: they must be heard and heeded lest the people be overtaken by judgment.

I had hoped that when Reverend Moon first proclaimed his message in the United States, it would be openly received by the American people and especially by the leaders of America's churches. His message could have elicited profound repentance and a new determination to overcome the sectarian and racial divisions in the churches, to overcome materialistic thinking, and to revive the original Christian spirit of selfless, giving love. It should have revived the central place of the family and encouraged superior morality and virtue as the foundation of a just and Godly society. It should have kindled America's idealism and sense of purpose so that this nation could fulfill its responsibility as the defender of freedom and source of strength to the world's developing countries who live under the threat of communist subversion. In so doing, America through this last decade could have been leading the way in building the multiracial, multinational, multicultural Kingdom of Heaven on the earth.

Unfortunately, at that time Reverend Moon was like a voice crying in the wilderness; only a very few Americans paid much attention to the words of this modern-day prophet. There was no widespread repentance, no reformation, no rekindling of idealism and purpose. God's hope that America could fulfill her divine calling was frustrated, and instead, America has drifted aimlessly for the last ten years. Reverend Moon's predictions of America's decline—increasing decadence and immorality, its loss of stature in the world, the fragmentation of society, and the loss of purpose and ideals—have come to pass.

A prophet is vindicated when his predictions are proven correct. At the very least, this republication of Reverend Moon's first proclamations to the American people can serve to chasten us and humble us to recognize that God is indeed speaking and working through this man. But no genuine prophet ever rejoices to see the fulfillment of his worst predictions of doom. His hope is always that the warnings might be heeded, that the people might repent, that God's will may be done. "As I live, says the Lord God, I have no pleasure in the death of the wicked, but that the wicked turn from his way and live; turn back from your evil ways" (Ezek. 33:11).

Once again, with this re-edition, I would hope the people of America come to recognize Reverend Moon's concern for the future of America. America is still at the crossroads where she must choose her direction; it is not too late for her to recover her purpose and take the path to renewed prosperity. Reverend Moon knows of God's love for America. He knows, too, that America cannot expect to prosper if she exists only for herself. America's future prosperity depends upon her taking responsibility to promote God-centered values, freedom and prosperity throughout the world.

I also hope that through these addresses, Christian leaders of all denominations can recognize God's and Jesus Christ's expectation for Christianity. God did not send Jesus Christ to this earth merely to save individuals that they may rest in their own private heaven. "For God so loved the *world* that He gave His only Son" means that Jesus came to save the entire world from evil and sin. Christians who truly know the will of God cannot, therefore, be content to remain separated into fractious and quarrelsome denominations, divided along doctrinal, racial, and ethnic lines. Indeed, God loves all the world's people, including those professing His name according to the tenets of non-Christian religions, and even those professing no religion who are working for goodness. Reverend Moon's message to all Christians is to wake up and recognize that Christianity's mission is to be seen in the context of God's greater providence to save the entire world.

Reverend Moon announces that the Kingdom of Heaven on earth is at hand, and that we are living at the time of the Second Coming of the Lord. The Lord comes not merely to vindicate those Christians who have been faithful and doctrinally pure. He comes rather to mobilize people to build the Kingdom of Heaven on the earth by living according to the spirit and love of Jesus Christ. Therefore, today, Christians will be judged not by the fervor of their individual faith, but by their contribution to the greater work of building God's kingdom. Those who remain bound to the narrow strictures of doctrine and tradition may miss the Lord when he appears, but those who are doing the will of God, who carry on the righteous struggle for God's Kingdom, and for whom the love of Christ is the highest aim, will have no difficulty in recognizing the Lord.

I have known Reverend Moon for over 30 years, and I can say without any reservation that, despite the many types of things he does, the most important aspect of his life is his deep spiritual connection to God. It is the first priority in his life. I know him as a man who has an insatiable appetite for a daily life of prayer. Up until this very day, he still sleeps less than three hours each day, and upon awakening, he begins each morning with several hours of prayer and meditation. For Reverend Moon, the affairs of the world cannot be considered without taking into account the presence of the Living God. Furthermore, through his study of the Bible and through his own prayer, he has realized that God's heart is filled with intense pain because human beings have not been able to understand God's situation. Likewise, Jesus has revealed to Reverend Moon his own painful grief and frustration because so few people have ever understood why he came or recognized the depth of his despair when he had to go to the cross. Ever since this understanding came to him, Reverend Moon's prayers have always been accompanied by tears.

Though I have shared many experiences with Reverend Moon, the image most deeply engraved in my heart is the image of him in prayer position, with tears streaming down his face. I have witnessed his spiritual life for many years, and I know him to be a righteous man who literally weeps for the suffering of God and the suffering of the world. He has committed his very life to the speedy establishment of peace and the Kingdom of God on this earth.

Reverend Moon has endured persecution throughout his life and has suffered imprisonment no less than five times

— once by the Japanese during World War II, twice by the North Korean Communists, once in South Korea for a trumped up draft evasion charge on which he was later cleared, and most recently in the United States. Although he was convicted in the United States on tax charges and imprisoned for thirteen months, Reverend Moon has received a tremendous outpouring of public support by Christian leaders, civil rights groups, scholars and politicians who recognized that he was the victim of unjust government persecution. He has never shirked persecution, firm in his belief that as long as he walks with God, every attack will ultimately rebound for the good.

The most striking impression I had of Reverend Moon through his trial and imprisonment was his remarkable attitude. Most people would have focused only on their personal misfortunes and become indignant at their mistreatment. Yet in prison, the first thing Reverend Moon did was to check himself and completely forgive the prosecutors, the judge and the government. Then he could go on with a clear mind to guide and inspire us and direct the activities of our movement as though nothing were amiss. Rather than being concerned about what was happening to him, he was fully occupied in the service of God.

Through all these years, Reverend Moon's faith has remained unwavering, his message clear and consistent. Although the speeches herein were Reverend Moon's first declarations to America, they remain as timely and necessary as ever. Their origin is God's revelation, which is firm and unchanging.

It is my hope, now that the controversy over Reverend Moon and his church has calmed somewhat, that you can take the time to consider his message. Reverend Moon did not come to America just to promote his church, but rather to proclaim the Word of God. It is this spiritual truth that has the power to save America and turn her from a course toward destruction. Like the words of the prophets of old, they are often hard words, and may be difficult for some people to accept. I humbly ask you to read with a sincere and prayerful heart, and then to inquire of God as to whether these words are true. Then, if you find truth in these words, please take up this vision as your own.

May God bless you.

Rev. Chung Hwan Kwak

God's Hope for Man

Lisner Auditorium, Washington, D.C.
October 20, 1973

Ladies and gentlemen, first of all I would like to express my heartfelt appreciation for your coming tonight. I thank God for this opportunity because I have been looking forward to visiting this city and meeting all of you.

Because we speak different languages, even though I can speak, from your standpoint I am dumb. And from my standpoint, even though you can hear, you are deaf. In order to correct this dumbness and deafness, we need the man standing next to me as my interpreter. However, as you know, interpretation from one language to another is not an easy task. So this man beside me really needs your sympathetic understanding.

My topic tonight is "God's Hope For Man." This subject is vast in nature and rather complicated in content. I will try my best to stay on the central point of my topic.

If there is a God, He definitely needs human beings. God created all things, but in all His creation man occupies the supreme and central position. It is therefore very important for us to have a clear understanding of the relationship between God and man. Historically, there have been many theories concerning this relationship. Varying opinions, theological concepts and academic schools abound, but the true, living relationship between God and man remains an unsettled question.

Because the relationship between God and man is so fundamental to life, our understanding cannot proceed until we have clarified this question thoroughly. As we pursue the answer, we discover that there are two main perspectives which we might take. One view is from God's standpoint, and the other is from man's point of view. Although various religions have developed through pursuing these two views, there must be one principle common to all religions which can clarify the relationship between God and ourselves. God wants us to understand this truth in its ultimate sense.

If somebody asks you, "What is the most precious thing in your life?" what will you answer? Some might say, "Power." Some would undoubtedly say money: "Money is everything." And others would suggest, "Wisdom or knowledge." Then, are those elements — power, money, knowledge—the most important things in life? When we look into this question deeply, other thoughts emerge. We soon come to the conclusion that the most precious thing is love; love is the most precious thing in life. And second to love, life itself is most precious. If we have love and life, we need one thing further—an ideal. These three elements—love, life, and an ideal—are not just precious and profound in value, they are the very things that make our lives worth living.

Let us consider something further. All men long for eternal life. By the same token, in our human expression of love and ideals, we feel an innate desire for them to be unchanging, unique, and everlasting. Many writers in history have described the beauty of the eternal kind of love. No writer has ever felt moved to glorify the kind of love that changes night and day. The many religions of the world which testify to a life beyond this earthly one support the reality of our desire for eternity. If a religion does not teach eternal life, that religion does not serve a good purpose.

Furthermore, the words "love" and "ideal" are without meaning by themselves. Love exists only when there is someone to love and someone to be loved by. An ideal needs to be shared with someone. Love and ideals come alive as soon as there is a reciprocal and complementary relationship of *give and take* established. We are in the position of the object and always need someone to be in the subject position. Love and ideals will bud and blossom into full flower only when two elements are in a subject-object relationship.

Is man the cause, the source of his universe, or did someone create us? How can man be the cause of the universe when he does not even create himself? It is obvious that we are resultant beings. We are the products of some cause. Therefore, a subject or cause must exist. There must be a cause for man's existence. This subject, or cause, then, is the essential reality. We should be as certain of this as we are of our own existence. Whatever name you choose for that cause doesn't matter. The most important things is that He is there. And we call him "God."

Let us put our question to God. "What is the most precious thing to you, God?" His reply will be no different from your answer and mine. God will answer, "Love, life, and my ideal are the most precious things to me." Does God need money? He created all things. Everything belongs to Him anyway. He does not need money. Does God need power? He is already the Source of all power. What about knowledge? God is omniscient and the Source of all knowledge. Yes, God is all these things; but He cannot have love, life, and His ideal all by Himself. He needs to share, to have give and take with someone in a reciprocal relationship. Even almighty God cannot experience the value of love, life and His ideal when He is alone. That is why God created His object, man.

Now I shall ask, "Why do we men act the way we do?" The answer is simple: because God acts that way. All human traits originate in God. Why are we the way we are? Because God is the way He is.

We are mirrors reflecting the characteristics of God. God is just like you and me. God is the Origin. Therefore, our love comes from the love of God. Our life comes from the life of God, and our ideals come from the ideal of God. We feel these are the most precious things because God first felt these things were most precious. God is the Subject of love, the Subject of life, and the Subject of ideals. We are the objects of love, the objects of life, and the objects of ideals. Therefore, if God is absolute, we are to be absolute. If God is unchanging, we are to be unchanging. If God is unique, we are to be unique. If God is everlasting, we are to be everlasting. Our eternal life is not just a fantasy. It is reality. Since God is eternal, His object, man, must be created for eternity. Otherwise, we cannot reflect the nature of our eternal God.

If there is a God of love, life, and ideals, and that God does not manifest all these qualities in man, His object, then

God has defeated His very purpose of creating. God either projected the full value of Himself in His object, or He created nothing at all. God is the Subject to man, and we are the objects to God. An object is the full reflection of the subject. So man is the visible form of God, and God is the invisible form of man. Subject and object are one in essence. God and man are one. *Man is incarnate God.* Otherwise, we would not be able to reflect God's full image. God could not realize His joy, the purpose of His creation. When we as objects are not as perfect as God Himself is perfect, we cannot reflect the full love, life, and ideal of God. So man, the object of God, is as important in value as God Himself.

If I made vigorous gestures and shouted to an empty auditorium, I am sure that anyone who saw me would wonder, "Is that man crazy?" But if I have someone to have give and take with, some object out there to respond to me — even one small child in front of me — and I pour out my heart and soul to him, then I am considered normal. The sole difference is the presence of someone as object. But let's say there is not even one little child in the audience. In desperation, I might pick up a little piece of dust, and looking at this dust, I could speak to it and still pour out my heart. Then I would at least not be a crazy man, for even a dust particle can serve as an object.

What I am trying to illustrate is the value of an object. As we are the objects to God, He has placed us in a position equal to Himself. Thus, man shares the same value as God and is just as important as God. Even though God is most high and noble and mighty, He too must have His object. Otherwise He feels no joy. Joy comes when you receive stimulation from the object. Not even God can be joyful alone. You must realize that God created man and the universe for joy. But God's joy remains dormant until He can have give and take with His object.

So far in Christianity, we placed God so high up in heaven, and pushed man so low in hell, that there has been an unbridgeable gap between them. A wide and raging river has separated man from God. Men do not dare to reach out to God as a living Reality. Man has been unable to realize that God is so close, so real, so approachable, that we can even dwell with Him. We are supposed to be the living temples of God. Yet conventional Christianity has been unable to make that a reality.

No matter how wealthy and famous you may be, unless you have someone with whom to have give and take so that you can share your joy, your sorrow, your opinions, and your ideals, you are just a poor man. We feel joy and sadness because God's heart can feel joy and sadness. Not until this time in history did we ever believe that God could feel sorrow. And God can feel excitement or indignation, just as we can. We, the objects of God, have this ability to experience emotion because our Subject, God, has the same capacity for emotion. God is the first Personality, and human personality comes from God. How then can we become true objects to God? By our efforts and hard work alone? No. There is but one way to come together in oneness with God. That way is through love—oneness in love with God.

Let me illustrate. Suppose there is a famous man. Opposite him is a woman who is unassuming and meek and without beauty or education. However, once this great man and this humble woman establish a circuit of give and take in love, she will instantly achieve his level of prestige. Let's say the man's name is Jones and he falls in love with this woman and marries her. She then becomes Mrs. Jones and returns his love with all her heart. Whatever power, authority and prestige Mr. Jones enjoys, Mrs. Jones would share in every respect. Now, what does this teach us? Once we have a relationship of love with God and become one with Him, our value increases instantly to the level of God's value. And such love as this is everlasting, unchanging, and unique.

Today is the time when we must fulfill this fundamental relationship between God and man. The subject and object must be one just as cause and effect are one. Therefore, the Bible says, "I am the Alpha and Omega, the beginning and the end, the first and the last" (Rev. 22:13). Within God, two are one. He is the beginning and we are the end. He is the first and we are the last. And the relationship between God and man is a circuit because beginning and end come together in oneness.

Peace, happiness and joy are the fruits of harmony in love. Therefore, in God's ideal of creation, He planned the relationship between God and man to be lived with harmony in love, with harmony in life, and with harmony in ideal.

Thus, we know that God is Subject and we are the objects. We also know that the object is just as important as the subject. We now want to know precisely what man's position as God's object means.

When God created man He gave him wisdom and ambition. Wisdom gives us the power to compare, and ambition gives us the power to strive for the best. If there are two choices before us, A and B, we will automatically compare them to determine which is better. Our human desire leads us to choose, and our ambition does not let us rest until we have obtained ultimate fulfillment.

Let me make another analogy. Let's say there is a most handsome man. He is not only handsome, but all-powerful and all-wise. You would be anxious to have some kind of personal relationship with this great man. What would you want it to be? Would you like to just be his servant? No, in your heart you know there is a position better than that of servant. Would you like to be only his friend? No, you would still not be happy. Would you like to be only his adopted son? Will this position bring you complete happiness? No, I don't think so. You would still crave some closer position. There is one relationship beyond which there is nothing more intimate. And that is to become a true son or daughter of this man. With this relationship you will have reached the ultimate fulfillment, and you cannot desire anything more.

Why, then, do we want to become true sons and daughters? Because that is the position in which to receive the man's love most fully. There is no closer or deeper relationship in human society than that between the father and son. Once you have your father's love, you possess everything he has. Every joy of the father, all the power of the father, all skill and wisdom and ambition and desire of the father — all will then be yours. In receiving the love of a father there is no procedure, neither paperwork nor ceremony, necessary to grant those things to a son. The father and son are automatically one. This principle applies among mankind, and it applies between man and God.

Then, what kind of relationship would you like to have with God? Would you be content to just be His servant? Or would you prefer to be His friend? Would you rather be His adopted son, or would you like to find a way to become God's own child? I know you will be satisfied with nothing short of the ultimate position as sons and daughters of God.

God's ultimate purpose in His creation of man is to give to him all His love, all His life, and all His ideal. You are to occupy the entire love of God, to the depth of His heart. By becoming His true sons and daughters, your desire will be fulfilled. That is your ultimate destiny. Then you will be saturated with the love of God. You will be filled with joy and feel overwhelmed by a total satisfaction in life.

There is no limit to joy. Happiness has no end. When you are standing in the love of God, every cell in your body jumps for joy. You breathe in and out with the entire universe. In this state your life is fulfilled. This is how God means us to live, intoxicated in love and joy. And through our joy, God receives His joy. The joy of man is the joy of God; the joy of God is the joy of man.

Early in my life God called me for a mission as His instrument. I was called to reveal His truth for Him, as His prophet. I committed myself unyieldingly in pursuit of truth, searching the hills and valleys of the spiritual world. The time suddenly came to me when heaven opened up, and I was privileged to communicate with Jesus Christ and the living God directly. Since then I have received many astonishing revelations. God Himself told me that the most basic and central truth of this universe is that *God is the Father and we are His children.* We are all created as children of God. And He said there is nothing closer, nothing deeper, nothing more intimate than when Father and son are one: one in love, one in life, and one in ideal.

Love, life, and ideal are at the central point where Father and son meet. Once we unite there, then God's love is our love; God's ideal is our ideal; God's life is our life. And there is no other relationship where you can have unity of life, unity of love, and unity of ideal any more than in the father-son relationship. This is a fundamental reality of the universe.

How do we come into being in this world? The father and mother become one through their love and bring together their lives and ideals. Their love precedes our birth. Love is the force which unites. Husband and wife become one in love. This means the husband's love, life, and ideal become the wife's, and the wife's love, life, and ideal become the husband's. This is the way that two live as one, and two become one flesh. Upon this foundation of oneness in love, a new life can be generated.

When a child is born, that child is the manifestation of his parents' love, life, and ideal. When you look at your own child, you are actually seeing another *you*. You are looking at the fruit of your love, the fruit of your life, and the fruit of your ideal. You are looking at your second self—another visible form of yourself.

Now let us expand this truth onto a universal scale. God created man and woman as His son and daughter. *He wants to see Himself in human beings.* Therefore, the Bible says, "God created man in his own image, in the image of God he created him; male and female he created them" (Gen. 1:27).

Man is created in the likeness of God. In other words, God made Himself incarnate in man. Man is the mirror of the living God, and His every virtue, characteristic, and quality is reflected in this mirror. God surely wants man to reflect His love, life, and ideal. Man is the fruit of God's love, life, and ideal.

How wonderful, how simply wonderful it is to live this perfected life of God! This is the true life of joy, unequalled by any earthly joy. Once you reach this state of perfection you don't need prayer. Why should you? You meet God face to face, and you live heart to heart with Him. You converse with God. You no longer need religion, and you don't need a savior. All these things of religion are part of the mending process, the process of restoration. A man of perfect health does not need a physician. The man in perfect union with God does not need a savior.

Life in union with God is the one great way to live— life with God, life in God, and God living in you. This was the spiritual state of Jesus when he said, "I am in the Father and the Father in me" (John 14:10). God and man will embrace in one all-consuming love. This is the state where God is made the living Reality. You no longer *believe*, but you *know*. And you *live* the truth. If you really experience this kind of love and oneness with God, then you have tasted the supreme experience of life. There are probably many Christian leaders among you, yet how many of you have had that wonderful experience, receiving the profound love of God?

God made man to live his life in intoxication. Man is meant to be intoxicated by the love of God. Since men lost this original capacity, they seek unnatural, artificial intoxication—getting drunk on alcohol, marijuana, or drugs. The perfect man, however, is created to be intoxicated in the love of God. There is nothing that can go beyond this feeling of joy. Every cell in your body will explode with joy. Your eyes and ears, the tissues in your face, your arms and legs —everything will be newly alive in a rapture of joy. Nothing else can ever match this quality of joy. This is the plan of God's original creation. When you say, "Heavenly Father," do you really have a living and vibrant feeling of God's presence? Don't you want to hear God answering, "Yes, my son?"

11

Here is my gift to you tonight: I want you to realize that the true relationship between God and man is a subject and object relationship. You are His sons and His daughters. Once you have achieved unity with God, nothing can trouble you. Neither sorrow nor loneliness, sickness or anything else under the sun can discourage you. God is the ultimate security. You could pay many millions of dollars and still not buy that kind of security. It is priceless. No money can buy it. This is the *total experience* of life. We are meant to live with God.

Your life is therefore the most valuable thing in this universe. That is why Jesus said, "For what will it profit a man, if he gains the whole world and forfeits his life? Or what shall a man give in return for his life?" (Matt. 16:26). Jesus is talking about life with God. Life without God is like a burned-out electric bulb which cannot give out light. A life without God is death.

Jesus Christ is the one man who lived God's ideal in its fullest realization. He was the first man of perfection ever to walk the earth, and he came to restore the true relationship between God and man. But after his crucifixion, Christianity made Jesus into God. This is why the gap between God and man has never been bridged. Jesus is a man in whom God is incarnate. But he is not God Himself. In the Bible, I Timothy 2:5 says, "For there is one God, and there is one mediator between God and men, the man Christ Jesus." The dwelling of God within Jesus was a total reality. He said, "I am in the Father and the Father in me" (John 14:10). Jesus is, indeed, the only begotten son of God, but God does not want *only* Jesus as His son. All mankind is created to be able to say, "I am in the Father and the Father in me." This is the fully attainable goal of everyone.

Our first step in becoming the true sons and daughters of God is to clearly comprehend God's view of good and evil. What is goodness and what is evil?

We are not concerned with a man-made definition. The eternal standard of good and evil is defined by God. The sharp definition of good and evil existed at the time of His creation, long before evil ever came into being in the Garden of Eden. God's view of good and evil will never change. God is eternal, His law is eternal, and His definition is eternal and unchanging despite the passage of time.

All of our human traits originate in God. We recognize that there is some human tendency for selfishness. This is natural because at one time God Himself was self-centered. This fact may surprise you, but you must understand that before God created man and the universe, He was *all alone,* with no one to care for except Himself. However, the very instant that God initiated creation, His full concept of life emerged. God now lives for His counterpart — not for Himself.

What is creation? Creation means nothing more than the Creator, God, projecting Himself into a substantial form. He made Himself incarnate symbolically in the universe, and He made Himself incarnate directly in man. When the spirit takes form, this is creation. God invested Himself in the creation. God's investment of energy *is* the creation.

The Bible in the book of Genesis makes creation sound simple and easy. Genesis gives us the impression that God's creation is accomplished through the magic of His words. God simply says, "Let there be a world," and presto!—the world comes into being. Then He says, "Let there be man," and poof!—Adam and Eve come into being.

But now it has been revealed that it was not this easy at all. God invested all of Himself in His creation. He did not reserve even one ounce of energy. Creation was His total labor, His total effort of giving all of Himself. When God put His entire heart and soul into the creation of His object, He was investing 100 percent of Himself. Only in this way could He create His second self, the visible God.

Therefore, after His creation God was no longer existing just for Himself. God began existing for His son and daughter, Adam and Eve. He exists to love, He exists to give. God is the totally unselfish existence. God cannot exist alone. "Love" and "ideal" only take on meaning when partners are in a complementary relationship. God initiated creation and made an investment He cannot lose. When God poured all of His love, life, and ideal into His second self, He had to, in a sense, realize a profit. God knew that when He invested all He had — 100 percent — His object would mature and return to Him many, many times over the fruits of love, life, and His ideal. His object, man, is everything to God. The life of the object attracts God. God wants to go and dwell with His object, man.

Let us look at an illustration. Suppose there is a great artist. If he works at random without feeling, he cannot create anything worthwhile. To create the masterpiece of his lifetime, the artist must put all of his heart and soul into his creation. That is the only way for him to come up with a great work of art. If an artist works in this way, his art becomes his life.

God is the greatest of all artists. When He created His masterpiece, man, He poured His heart into the process. He poured His soul into it. He poured all of His wisdom and all of His energy into it. God wished only to exist for Adam and

Eve and all mankind. He saved not a single ounce of energy when He created them. Thus, man has become the life of God.

God set a pattern for the universe. In the ideal existence, we live for others. The subject exists for the object and the object exists for the subject. God's definition of goodness is total giving, total service, and absolute unselfishness. We are to live our lives for others. You live for others and others live for you. God lives for man and man lives for God. The husband lives for his wife and the wife lives for her husband. This is goodness. And here unity, harmony and prosperity abound.

Would you, as a man, be disturbed if I said that you were created for a woman? Perhaps some of you are proud of your masculinity and would not want to hear this. But this is the principle of God's creation, and you must not be sorry to hear these words. Man lives his life for his partner, not for himself.

Let us assume that one of you ladies is a beauty queen. No matter how beautiful you are, your beauty is not for your own gratification; it is for the delight of men. We are created to live for each other. This is the very reason for our existence; we exist for others, for an object, for a counterpart. This is the principle for all human relationships in our society. Parents exist for their children, and children exist for their parents. Then both parents and children, when they give unselfishly, become united in a circular motion.

This circling motion is the motion of unity. When you give and take, the give and take action creates a circular motion. Circular motion alone can be eternal, because there you will find no end. Therefore, all of God's creation is based on a pattern of circular movement, since He created for eternity. Even our faces are round, although there is one central vertical line. Our eyeballs are round, and there are upper and lower lips which make up a round mouth. The sun is round, the moon, the earth, and all heavenly bodies are round. They are each rotating on their own axes and revolving around others. Everything in this universe has complementary give and take action between subject and object. Give and take action occurs between artery and vein, and thus blood circulates through the body. Human sickness is the state where the balance of give and take action is broken, and normal circulating motion is stopped. Without having this give and take action between subject and object, without abiding by this principle, nothing endures for eternity. All existence that is based upon God's principle is a good existence.

Then, what is evil? Evil is the emergence of selfishness into this world. God's principle of unselfish giving was twisted into an ungodly principle of selfish taking. The ungodly position of desiring to be served rather than to serve was thereby established. The origin of evil is Satan. He was in the position to serve God, but instead he posed as another god and subjugated man for his own benefit. God is the absolute positive force in this universe. Then Satan posed as another positive force. Two positives naturally repel each other. Satan is a fallen archangel. He left his position as faithful servant to God and man, and he challenged and competed with God. *His motivation was selfishness.* Out of his selfishness comes the origin of evil and sin.

What happened was this: Eve fell from her position as God's first daughter, becoming the first victim of Satan and transforming herself into a creature of selfishness. Together Eve and Satan then successfully brought Adam into their selfish world. By this tragic event, God was isolated by man in the Garden of Eden. Human history started on the wrong footing, without God. The foundation for the evil history of man was laid, and Satan was established as the ruler of this world. Selfishness came into being at the beginning of human history, and now our world is rampant with killing, lying and stealing. All of these actions in the evil world are motivated by selfishness. Evil subjugates others for its own benefit, while good sacrifices itself for the benefit of others.

Since the fall of man, God's work has been the restoration of original goodness. God wants to destroy the world of evil and recreate the world of goodness. We have lost our health. We have become sick people. The salvation of God is, therefore, the restoration of man to a healthy state once again.

God sowed the seed of goodness, but before He could gather its fruit, Satan invaded with his evil seed and harvested his evil fruit. For this reason, God must sow the seed of goodness once again. To do this job, God needs certain tools. The religions of the world have served as these tools for God. Throughout history, good religions have taught God's way of life, centered upon sacrificial love and duty. Thus Christianity may be considered the most advanced and progressive religion because it teaches this sacrificial love and duty in supreme form.

Jesus came as a savior, but his teaching was, "The Son of man came not to be served but to serve" (Matt. 20:28). Jesus taught that the greatest love in this universe is to give one's life for his enemy. The teaching of the Bible is contrary to the common rule of our worldly society. It is exactly the opposite of the way of this self-centered world. The Bible teaches complete giving and total sacrifice. "He who finds his life will lose it, and he who loses his life for my sake will find it" (Matt. 10:39). It seems almost foolish to think seriously about living this way in man's evil society. But once you know God's principle, you discover that there is actually no wisdom greater than this.

Jesus Christ's teachings were hitting at the very core of this fundamental truth. The more you give the more you receive. God rewards total giving with total love, and total sacrifice with total life. Giving creates room for God's love to enter. The more room and the greater the vacuum created by your giving, the faster you will be filled by the flow of God's love.

To be treated well you must first treat others well. You reap as you sow. Sow evil to reap evil; sow goodness to reap goodness. Your concern should be how to give, and how to give well. As for the return to you, you must trust in God. He will take care of it.

Let us take an illustration of a good man and a bad man. Let us say there is one man who has ten friends. Day in and day out this man is unselfishly serving his ten friends. People cannot help but love this man. He can become the very best friend to ten people. Then his influence will spread to the relatives and friends of those first ten people. By giving and serving unselfishly, this man becomes prosperous. He is a center of harmony and unity because he lives God's principle. Unselfishness brings prosperity. Here is a good man.

But suppose, on the contrary, this man said to his friends, "You ten, bring everything to me; you are here to serve me." Before he could speak this way to his friends three times, everyone would end all connection with him. They would want to have nothing at all to do with him. Soon he would be left all alone. Isn't that true, even in our society? It is universally true: A self-centered doctrine, a self-centered philosophy, a self-centered way of life will fling you head over heels down the tragic road of self-destruction. But if you will live your life in service to others, you will find prosperity. It may seem that such a route would lead you to ruin, but it will not. The only reason it may not always bring prosperity to you is because you do not give to the very end. In the middle, you suddenly become skeptical. You change your heart or pity yourself and thus shrink from God's law of total giving. The good result never materializes. Total giving is the way of prosperity because it is the way of God.

If any individual sacrifices himself for another individual, he becomes a hero to others. If one family is sacrificial for the well-being of another family, then that family becomes a heroic family among all families. Peoples and nations who sacrifice themselves for the benefit of others become champions of nations. A man who gives his life for his parents is a pious son. A man who gives his life for his king is a loyal subject. And a man who gives his life for all mankind is a saint.

Jesus Christ proclaimed this very truth you are hearing tonight. He strove for the fulfillment of God's truth on earth. He came not to satisfy his nation's selfish purpose, but to achieve salvation for the entire world.

God intended the chosen people of Israel to serve as the prepared instrument of the Messiah for his mission of world salvation. The people of Israel did not know this. They conceived of the coming Messiah as an invincible military conqueror who would restore the political empire of King David for the glory of the Jews. How wrong they were!

God's purpose is not the salvation of any particular man, church, or nation. God's purpose is to save the whole world. Therefore, the true church would give itself as a sacrifice for the benefit of the world. Yes, true Christians must be willing to sacrifice their own lives for the salvation of the world and all mankind. However, Christian teachings today are self-centered. Christians are seeking their own personal salvation. Christians are crying out for "my salvation" and "my heaven." This is contrary to God's truth and contrary to God's ideal. We must steadfastly give, love, sacrifice, and live for the sake of others.

We must all work for the ideal way of life. I exist for my family, my family exists for our society, our society exists for our nation, our nation exists for the world, all the world exists for God, and God exists for you and me, for all mankind. In this great circle of give and take, there is harmony, there is unity, and there is an eternal process of increasing prosperity. Furthermore, since in this circuit all existence will fulfill its purpose of creation, there is abundant and profound joy. This is the Kingdom of Heaven, in which feelings of happiness overflow.

In this world, selfishness ruins everything. Selfishness in the family causes disharmony, which then erupts into bitterness and strife. Everyone wants to be served instead of serving others. Wives tell their husbands what to do and then seek to be served. Husbands want to be served by their wives. Parents expect service from their children, and the children take their parents for granted. This is demonstrated in our families, in our societies, and in our nations.

In this world today, the nations are existing solely for their own national interests. They plot, connive, cheat, and lie. They destroy other nations for their own national benefit.

Is there even one nation on earth which pledges to God, "God, you may use this nation as your sacrifice and as your altar, if that is the way you can save the world"? Tell me, where is such a nation? Where?

It is a recognized fact that when America demonstrated the spirit of service and sacrificial duty in the world and went out of her way to help others in their need—when America gave lives, money, and a helping hand — she enjoyed a golden age. But now America has a selfish attitude. The domestic problems today are very difficult. America's situation is chaotic. Today there are greater division, more corruption, and graver problems choking this land.

I am not criticizing any people or any nation. I am merely proclaiming the heavenly truth that all mankind is seeking.

I started the Unification Church. If this Unification Church exists solely for the benefit or the welfare of the Unification Church itself, then it is doomed to perish. I founded the Church so that I could give my life, my heart, and my soul for the advancement of the salvation of the world. Among this audience there are many members of the Unification Church. Their great desire, their only motivation is to serve others, to save this nation and the world.

Jesus did not teach his disciples laws of retaliation. He told them, "If anyone strikes you on the right cheek, turn to him the other also; ...and if anyone forces you to go one mile, go with him two miles" (Matt. 5:39-41). You never have to retaliate; all you have to do is completely and totally give, and then God will return to you more and more abundantly.

When Jesus was crucified, Roman soldiers pierced him. And Jesus prayed for his enemies: "Father, forgive them; for they know not what they do" (Luke 23:34). Even at the moment of death on the cross, Jesus was so earnest in forgiving. His very last act was motivated by his love for his enemies. He was the supreme form of giving — a paragon of love. The example of Jesus Christ is the absolute standard for all mankind. Just imagine an entire nation composed of Jesus-like men. What would you call it? The Kingdom of Heaven on earth — it could be nothing less.

Jesus Christ was lord over all life because of his unparalleled form of loving, giving, and sacrifice. He will remain the Lord forever. In the same way, no one in this universe surpasses the total giving and loving of God. So God is God forever. He reigns over all creation.

Look at the decline of Rome. The entire Roman Empire collapsed in front of the army with no weapons, the army of Jesus Christ. By what means did the Christians conquer Rome? They conquered by love, sacrifice, and total giving, up to the cost of their very lives. History is witness that no empire can withstand the army of sacrificial love. And this history shall be repeated.

Up to now in our lives, we did not know clearly the definition of good and evil. We could not be certain where to commit ourselves, when to act, what to serve. This has been the source of the greatest confusion in human lives. We must not become the Christians who merely crave their own well-being. As Christians, we must live the life of Jesus and give ourselves totally for the benefit of others so that others might have life. This is God's way.

This present world is evoking the wrath of God. It truly deserves His uncompromising judgment. But God is love, and He is long-suffering. God is suppressing His anger because He wants to save us. He is giving us a chance to change. He is waiting.

I know that Western culture is characterized by individualism. However, *selfish* individualism is doomed. *Sacrificial* individualism will blossom. Individuality in itself is good. God gave each one of us a unique way to serve. But individualism without God can only build castles on the sands of decay.

I can see a great change, a great new surge of revolution coming to America—not by fire, not by bullets, but by God's truth kindling a revolution of men's hearts. I have come here to ignite this spiritual revolution. I don't need to demonstrate in front of the White House or in Lafayette Square. The answer does not lie there, but in the hearts of men, in the quiet revolution from selfishness to unselfishness.

Can you imagine how wonderful the ideal society will be? Individuals will belong to their families, the families will belong to the society, society will belong to the nation, the nation will belong to the world, the world will belong to God, and God will belong to you. He who gives the most will know God most deeply.

Some young people might say to me, "Rev. Moon, you are coming here repeating the same old stuff." But that is not at all true. I am speaking not from theory but from life. I am telling you that we are all here to live the truth, as Jesus lived the truth. This is not a theory, a philosophy, or a theological doctrine. It is the ultimate truth of God—not to be talked about, but *to be lived*.

When man makes this truth live, it is going to bring about the greatest change upon the face of the earth. Although in one sense you know the truth of the things I have been saying, still nobody ever lives it. This truth is as old as God, yet as new as the 21st century. You must live the truth. If the revelation of the Divine Principle has made this age-old truth real in your heart, then you have in effect discovered a brand-new truth. The Divine Principle is touching the hearts of millions of young people, showing them the way to our very real God. People throughout the world are learning that God is absolute and perfect, and perfect God demands perfect man as His object. Jesus said, "You, therefore, must be perfect as your heavenly Father is perfect" (Matt. 5:48). He is clearly indicating that our standard of value is the perfection of our heavenly Father. Otherwise we cannot be God's objects and God cannot accept us.

All of us want to be perfect. All of us want heaven on earth, but we ask, "How can it be done?"

We wonder if it is at all possible for man to be perfect. Some contend, with apparent justification, that all one has to do is merely look at man to see the gross error of such an aspiration. We point to the sin and suffering inherent in all things, even in the things that are most holy. We say, "Only God is perfect." However, when we fully comprehend the design for man in God's concept of creation, we will understand that perfection is within our grasp.

In God's ideal of creation, we were designed as temples of God, temples of the spirit of God, where God is master. "Do you not know that you are God's temple and that God's spirit dwells in you?" (I Cor. 3:16).

We were designed to be God's temples. When we attain this status, we shall cease to possess a will that is corruptible. Limitations or laws will no longer be necessary, for His will is our will. With His spirit dwelling in us completely we shall move only as He dictates. We shall then be perfect because the force that is guiding and directing us is the perfect force.

When man achieves this ultimate goal he is in perfect union with God. He is no longer living on the human level alone, but on the God-like level. He takes on God's qualities because the Spirit dwells in and possesses him as a perfect temple; he reflects God's virtue and power. Thus man can be as perfect as the heavenly Father is perfect. This was the original pattern which God intended for mankind through Adam.

Marriage is the most important means of establishing God's kingdom on earth. Adam and Eve were God's first children. They were born of God, grew up in God, and would have matured into perfection in God. God intended to make Adam and Eve one in heavenly matrimony. Then they would have borne sinless children and become the true father and mother for all mankind. They would have been the first "king" and "queen," establishing the heavenly kingdom on earth.

Has such a kingdom ever existed? No. Instead, history started in the wrong direction. From the evil first step, Satan has been the god of this world. It has, therefore, been God's purpose of restoration, His purpose of salvation, to restore the perfected nation so that He can truly have His kingdom upon the earth. For this God needs a model. Who can set the criteria of perfection on this earth? *To meet this need, the Messiah comes.*

Jesus Christ came as the Messiah. He was the model of perfection upon every level: the individual, family, tribal, national, and worldwide levels. He came to establish a perfect world in his lifetime, not over a period of centuries.

Before God sent His champion, Jesus Christ, He prepared the field with the chosen people of Israel. They were the foundation for the Messiah's coming. The people of Israel could have perfected themselves and their nation if they had united with the coming of the Lord. The kingdom of God would have been a physical reality at that time.

But Jesus was not accepted by his people. Instead of welcome, he met rejection at every level. Jesus was denied the opportunity to take a bride in the position of restored Eve and to establish the first God-centered heavenly family. Instead, he was nailed to the cross. Read I Corinthians 2:8: "None of the rulers of this age understood this; for if they had, they would not have crucified the Lord of glory." Thus, the mission of Jesus Christ was left undone on earth.

The history of God's providence is a sad, sad story. To comfort the heart of God and fulfill His work, we must clearly understand His process of restoration.

When God created man, He placed Adam and Eve, man and woman, in the Garden of Eden. They both united with Satan and became sinful, thereby leaving God isolated. In the process of restoration, God must restore both Adam and Eve. Jesus came as the sinless Adam, or perfected Adam. His first mission was, therefore, to restore his bride and form the first family of God. All fallen generations would have been grafted onto him as the true olive tree. God-centered families, tribes, and nations would thus have been restored. Perfection would have reigned. The sinless state of God's kingdom could have been a reality for the last 2,000 years. This is why I Corinthians 15:45 says Jesus is the "last Adam," the second Adam.

Jesus came, but he was crucified. He was not given the chance to restore his bride. And this is why Jesus promised his second coming. Jesus Christ must come again to consummate the mission he left undone 2,000 years ago. Let me repeat: Jesus was the perfected Adam, and his mission was the restoration of mankind. The first step was to restore his bride, Eve. Jesus was a man, not God Himself. When he returns to earth, he will come as a man in the position of the third Adam.

Let us understand more fully the significance of these revelations. In the book of Revelation, there is the prophecy of the marriage of the Lamb. God intended Adam and Eve to come together in heavenly matrimony in the Garden of Eden. Since it was not realized at that time, God intended Jesus to fulfill this marriage in his time. But it was not realized by Jesus either because of the faithlessness of the chosen people.

Jesus was the second Adam. It was God's will for him to be blessed in heavenly matrimony with the second Eve, his restored bride. God intended him to bring forth upon this earth his own sinless children. Then Jesus and his bride would have become the True Parents for mankind. And all mankind would have found life by grafting onto them.

Jesus cautioned the people: "You are of your father the devil" (John 8:44). Because of the beginning point of human history, we were born as Satan's children. By the restoration of True Parents, we will be reborn as children of our Heavenly Father, God, with full salvation into His sonship.

God's will was denied fulfillment in Jesus' time. That is why he is coming again as the third Adam. The marriage supper of the Lamb will take place. True Parents for all mankind will be realized in our time. God will bring forth His true family upon the face of the earth. All men will be made new through their True Parents. All will be made capable of bringing sinless children into the world. This will be done when Jesus Christ reappears. The Kingdom of Heaven on earth will then begin. This will be the day of hope, the day of the coming of the Lord of the Second Advent.

This is the day when God's original ideal will be realized for the first time. This is the day when the dwelling of God is with men. God will be full of joy. His own son as perfected third Adam will initiate an entirely new history upon the earth. On that day, we shall become living images of God. God will bring His kingdom to earth.

I pledge to you from the bottom of my heart that the realization of all this is at hand, in the fullness of God's time. The ultimate realization of this ideal has been the hope of God as well as the hope of man.

Thank you very much for your attentive listening. You have been a most gracious audience. Thank you.

God's Hope for America

Lisner Auditorium, Washington, D.C.
October 21, 1973

Ladies and gentlemen, I would like to express once again tonight my thanks for your coming to my lecture. My topic tonight is "God's Hope For America."

I love all of you very much because I love God—and God loves America and the American people.

It has been a cardinal principle of God's providence that in order to receive God's blessing you must first demonstrate your worthiness of the blessing. Throughout history there have been many righteous people who demonstrated their worthiness of God's blessing by leading sacrificial lives. Nevertheless, we know that the world we live in today is not literally God's kingdom. We learn that human history started on the wrong footing, on the evil side. This is why the Bible says that the god of this world is Satan.

It has been the strategy of God to summon champions out of this evil world in order to restore the world and build

His kingdom. To understand His ways, let us therefore examine the history of God's providence. The family of Adam was the first family in God's creation. In this family there was a man, Abel, whom God chose to be His first champion. Abel served God wholeheartedly and became the first man to give up his life for God's purpose.

Later on God called Noah as the champion. And Noah accomplished a very unusual mission. God directed Noah to build a ship, and he was to build it on top of a mountain. Now, it is just common sense that in building a ship you need a shipyard by some body of water. But Noah's instructions were to build the ark on top of a mountain rather than at the seashore or riverside. How many of us here could accept that kind of mission? How many of us could obey such a command and set to work without a single shred of doubt?

In Noah's time, no one could believe that Noah had received a command from God—nor did anyone accept him in his mission of revealing the coming flood judgment. Can you imagine how Noah appeared to the people of his day? For 120 years he went up and down, up and down that mountain working on his boat. Would anyone among the ladies in the audience like to think of herself in the position of the wife of Noah? I don't think you would be a very happy wife.

Noah's wife must have packed his lunch basket every day, using only a little food. Noah was so busy with the ark he could not find time to provide for his family. Within a few months the family squabbles must have begun, but it was not just for twelve months or twelve years that Noah's wife had to sustain her situation, but for 120 years. Why, then, did God ask of Noah such an incomprehensible mission? Why does God have to work that way? There is a reason. It is because of evil.

God cannot dwell together with evil. The direction of God is 180 degrees contrary to the direction of evil. God abhors evil. God cannot accept the things that the evil world accepts. So God does not want anything to do with the evil world or with whatever is tainted by evil.

We are all in the image of God and can find traits similar to His in our human nature. Consider if you have an enemy toward whom you have strong feelings; you don't want to so much as look at that person. Likewise, God will have nothing to do with the evil, Satanic world. Therefore, in dealing with it, He chooses ways often incomprehensible to man.

God also tests the faith of man. He cannot do this by asking just ordinary things of people. We must be willing to comply with God's extraordinary instructions. We must display to God absolute faith. This is not an easy task. People thought Noah was a crazy man for building the ark. Nobody knew he occupied the central position in God's view.

Not only Noah, but other men of God seem to act in peculiar ways when they are seen from the worldly viewpoint. Let us take a look at Abraham.

God summoned Abraham, not from a family headed by a man of God, but from an idol-maker's house, and ordered him to separate himself from his evil surroundings and leave his homeland. God wanted Abraham to be his champion. This was God's personal command. If Abraham had then discussed this matter with his father, the idol-maker would undoubtedly have asked him, "Are you crazy?" Abraham knew better than to mention anything to his father about his instructions from God. Who would have believed him? His mission was not just to say hello to his next door neighbor. God instructed him to journey to a strange land, as far away as Egypt.

Abraham's decision then was a lonely one, based upon his faith and his reliance upon God. I know he stole away in the middle of the night. Suddenly he found himself wandering like a gypsy. He lived in self-denial; he had given up everything.

The champions of God have one characteristic in common: They begin their missions by denial of themselves and their surroundings. Isaac's son, Jacob, was no exception. Jacob was a man with strong willpower in service to God. He wanted to serve God in an unprecedented fashion. He wanted to open an exemplary path, accomplishing something nobody else could duplicate.

In the Bible there are many stories about Jacob. One describes a very cunning act when he bought his elder brother's birthright in exchange for a bowl of pottage. And later on he stole his father's blessing, which was intended for his elder brother Esau. In this incident Jacob knew beyond any doubt that he would make an enemy out of his elder brother. He committed himself nonetheless. That craving in Jacob, that ardent desire for God's blessing, was so strong in his heart that God was really comforted. After obtaining Isaac's blessing, Jacob then escaped the danger of being killed by his elder brother when he fled from his homeland and went to the strange land of Haran.

For 21 years Jacob endured a life of tribulation in Haran. During that time Jacob was repeatedly deceived by his uncle Laban. Ten times Laban cheated Jacob, and Jacob did not complain even once. He just persevered and waited for the day when he could return to his blessed homeland.

That day finally came, and at the ford of Jabbok, on the way back, God sent an angel to fight with Jacob. Now consider this: An angel from God suddenly appeared to Jacob and became a dreadful enemy. God was really pressing Jacob and testing the strength of his faith. Jacob had to wrestle with the angel. And he did wrestle.

Jacob didn't cease fighting all through the night. He never gave up. And then God knew that Jacob's determination was to fight to the end, even to death. Even when the angel hit his thigh bone and knocked it out of joint, Jacob still did not give up despite the pain. Jacob finally won the test. The angel of God surrendered, and said to him, "Your name shall no more be called Jacob, but Israel, for you have striven with God and with men, and have prevailed" (Gen. 32:28).

Later on God chose Moses as His champion. Imagine how fortunate Moses was to grow up in the Pharaoh's palace, where he could enjoy a luxurious life. But then one day as a young man he suddenly stood up as the champion of his people; he could no longer stand the Egyptians' oppression of his people. At that moment he knew that God was with him. He rejected his surroundings, denied himself, and went to the wilderness of Midian. He awaited his ultimate mission for forty years, persevering and growing worthy of God's blessing. Moses' life was very humble and meek. Every day he surrendered himself anew to God's purpose and asked His divine guidance, eagerly awaiting his eventual mission, the leading of his people out of Egypt.

These men—Abel, Noah, Abraham, Jacob, and Moses —were champions of God. Now let us look also at John the Baptist. Described in the Bible as a great saint and prophet, John the Baptist went around the countryside like a common vagabond. He went without shoes, wearing camel skin with a leather belt, sustaining himself on locusts and wild honey. This was not a customary way to live, even in John's time; and I don't think John the Baptist's parents were very proud of their son. They must have felt ashamed.

Suppose you put yourself in the position of parents with your son, John the Baptist, going out in the wilderness year after year and living like a beggar. How would you feel? I have traveled in Israel, and I don't believe you will find many locusts or much wild honey in the desert. John the Baptist had to beg for his food many times. Imagine him wearing a camel skin, half of his body exposed, barefoot, and with a beard, going from one place to another begging for food. If I came up here on the podium tonight barefoot, with a beard and clothed in an animal skin, and then said I was proclaiming the word of God, I am sure you would think I was crazy.

Let us continue along this line and examine the situation of Jesus Christ himself. I am sure there are many devout Christians among you who have various opinions on the life of Jesus. How would you visualize Jesus' appearance? What was Jesus doing for the thirty years before his public ministry? Was he in a college studying? The Bible doesn't say he even went to elementary school. He was a laborer, an assistant to a carpenter. There is so much to know, so many hidden truths within the Bible which are not written explicitly. If I revealed some of those secrets, I am sure you would be amazed. Even though I know these things, I could not tell you those stories lightly. For you would then ask, "How do you know such things?"

I learned them from Jesus. Yes, and I learned from God. Remember, at the time of Noah nobody could believe

Noah. At the time of Abraham, nobody could believe Abraham. By the same token, even though I will honestly tell you what actually happened at the time of Jesus, no one will easily believe me.

From the point of view of the society of those days, Jesus was a fatherless child, an illegitimate child. In the sight of God he was conceived by the Holy Spirit, but there was no way to prove it to people! So set your thoughts in a realistic vein and just evaluate what I am going to say.

Mary conceived Jesus before marriage. Under the Jewish law, such a woman was to be condemned to death by stoning. Joseph suffered indignation because of Mary's situation, and quietly waited for the right time to break the engagement. Then an angel appeared to Joseph and said to him, "You are to take Mary as your wife. Do not condemn her, for she has a special mission from God." If Joseph had not been a righteous man, Mary would have been automatically condemned to death by stoning.

Now, do you think Joseph could have discussed this matter with his parents by saying, "Mother and Father, my wife-to-be, my betrothed, has conceived a child, but an angel said that this is the will of God, so I must take her as my wife and care for her"? What would Joseph's parents have said? There are many older couples in our audience. Put yourselves in the position of the parents of Joseph. You would not have believed Joseph if he spoke such things. Again, Joseph had to make a lonely decision. Without discussing the matter with anybody, he took his fiancee off to some secret hiding place.

I am sure Joseph went through a most difficult period in which he was full of suspicion about Mary. Joseph must have asked his wife-to-be, "Mary, we are close and have no secrets from one another. Now tell me what really happened to you. Who is the true father of the baby in your womb?" I am sure any husband would be very curious about this matter. If I had been in the position of Joseph, I would have asked Mary this question. But Mary was telling the truth when she said, "I really do not know who is the father of this child. It was conceived by God." How many of us could believe her statement? It is easier to believe now, because we know who Jesus is, but this was not the case during the lifetime of Jesus.

Therefore, Joseph had certain suspicions and injured feelings in his heart. He thought, "My wife is not truly honest with me." Because of these circumstances, there was emotional turmoil and upheaval in Jesus' family even after he was born.

One instance in particular witnesses to this fact. One day Jesus met his mother at a wedding feast in Galilee, and Mary informed Jesus that they had run out of wine. He called out to his mother, saying, "Woman, what have you to do with me?" (John 2:4). The point is, he did not say, "Mother," but instead called out, "Woman." Later on a disciple of Jesus came to him saying, "Your mother and your brothers would like to see you." And Jesus replied, "Who are my mother and my brothers?... Here are my mother and brothers! Whoever does the will of God is my brother, and sister, and mother" (Mark 3:33-35). This indicates that in the eyes of Jesus the members of his family were not doing the will of God.

Jesus suffered great anguish within his own family. There are many hidden stories not yet revealed. Many of the facts about his suffering are unknown. The Bible leaves a scanty record of the thirty years before Jesus' public ministry. If this were a glorious record, we can be sure that God and Jesus' disciples would have revealed it. But Jesus lived in sorrow and grief; he was an obscure figure for thirty years. People were therefore shocked one day when they heard him say, "I am the fulfillment of the Law," and "Moses wrote of me." He proclaimed, "I am the Son of God," and "The Father in heaven has sent me." "I am the Way, the Truth, and the Life; no one comes to the Father but by me." How many of us could have accepted such extraordinary statements if we had lived in those days? Jesus just bewildered people, he sounded so outrageous. Even John the Baptist had difficulty seeing Jesus as the Son of God, and John was supposed to come to prepare the people and make straight the way of the Lord.

Today it is very easy to accept Jesus Christ as the Son of God, because for 2,000 years Christianity has been glorifying him as God. But in those days, the elders did not accept. And the priests did not accept him either. They were no less intelligent than we are today. In fact, we would probably have compounded their mistakes if we had lived in the days of Jesus of Nazareth. They saw only an outcast, a blasphemer, and an outrageous heretic. They simply could not see the Son of God.

Jesus had been long awaited. The Messiah was expected for 2,000 years. But when he finally appeared, there was no reception for him. The faith of the Jews at that time was no less powerful, no less devout than the faith of Christians today. Yet we know that the people Jesus associated with were not on a par with the rest of society, that he mixed with harlots, tax collectors, and fishermen. We know the story that one day a young woman poured precious ointment over Jesus' body, then washed his feet with her hair. If we had seen these things, how many of us can say in a pious manner that we would have accepted Jesus as the Son of God?

The three years of Jesus' public ministry were a far cry from the anticipated Messiahship. No one understood Christ's true mission. The people judged the Son of God with sinful eyes, according to their own earthly standards. And they treated him as they pleased. This sinful world can never be hospitable to the purity of Christ. He came to his own people but the people received him not.

As I mentioned, all the saints and prophets and righteous men of history had first to deny themselves totally and give themselves up to God. When He summoned them, they gave up their homes, their fortunes, their families and their nations. God wants His champion on the individual level, on the family level, tribal level, national level and worldwide level. He has summoned His champions on each level. And the qualification for God's champion on any level always remains the same. He needs the absolute and untiring faith required to follow His command wherever it may lead. God needs total obedience to His will.

We must examine, then, what the will of God is. Why does He give His people such a hard time? Individual salvation is certainly important in the sight of God. God does not neglect that. However, that is not the ultimate purpose of God's work. God's will is the salvation of the world! God needs an individual to be His champion for the ultimate goal of world salvation. God summoned one family to be an instrument for the salvation of the world. God summoned His people to achieve the salvation of the world. God wants to have a nation as His champion for the ultimate fulfillment of world salvation.

People in the time of Jesus were anxiously awaiting the Messiah. But they were thinking only of their own national glory as Israel, the chosen people of God. They did not understand the universal mission of Jesus Christ. It was the purpose of God to send the Messiah to the chosen people of Israel so that they would unite with him. Then they could become soldiers of faith, to fight for and achieve the salvation of the world.

The foundation for the Messiah was laid through Jacob, the champion of the family, and through Moses, the champion of his people. Finally, the Messiah came to the nation of Israel. He was to be the champion of the nation and the champion of the entire world. The purpose of God is not the salvation of one church or one nation alone. It is the will of God that He sacrifice the lesser for the greater. Therefore He will sacrifice the church or the nation for the world. If Christians today think only of their own salvation, their own heaven and their own well-being, then they are not living in accordance with the purpose of God. If we are only concerned with the salvation of our own families, we are not worthy of God's blessing. If people focus on benefiting their own people alone, or their nation alone, then they are absolutely going against the will of God.

God will give you your own salvation. When you become God's champion for world salvation, your own salvation is guaranteed. Now, the Christian population is probably one-seventh of the total world population. But among these, very few are devout Christians. And among devout Christians, how many of us really strive for the salvation of mankind? We must all devote ourselves to the salvation of the world!

God cannot be pleased with man if we live in a self-centered way. I met Jesus personally, and I received a revelation through which I learned that God's grief is great. His heart is broken. Today, God is working ceaselessly for the ultimate salvation of all mankind. He needs His champion to succeed in this work. The purpose of God's church is to save the entire world. The church is the instrument of God, and it was this very fact that the chosen people of Israel forgot at the time of Jesus.

Beginning with this knowledge, let us now continue our historical perspective and determine how America has become blessed.

After Jesus' crucifixion and glorious resurrection, the Christian church spread throughout Asia Minor. The principal thrust was Rome. Rome was the target because at that time Rome was "the world." For the world to be saved, Rome had to be conquered by the army of Jesus Christ. But this was an impossible battle, an inconceivable goal. The Roman Empire appeared as an impregnable fortress not subject to conquest. Jesus' army was barehanded. They used no weapons, neither swords nor spears. They were armed only with their love of God and Jesus Christ. They marched fearlessly onward, in conviction and strength. They paid the price in blood and sacrifice.

There can be no stronger army than the one which fears no death. No enemy is invincible against an army of faith. History is witness to the deeds of that army of Jesus. The Roman Empire fell at last, and Jesus conquered Rome. Roman Catholicism became the center of God's dispensation of world salvation. The Pope was in the position to become God's champion.

However, in the Middle Ages, great corruption appeared in the church, and Christianity disintegrated in spirit. Medieval church hierarchies were interested in their own power, their own authority, and their own welfare. The church enjoyed formidable power both politically and economically. The hierarchy preserved this power, abused this power, and forgot about God's purpose. They clung tenaciously to their positions and ruthlessly persecuted any opponent. The church leaders claimed lineage from Jesus' disciples, yet they could not rise above their own sins. The Christian spirit in these men was absolutely dead.

But God had to continue forward. He is never satisfied with less than a total response. The church needed reform, so religious revolution came. Martin Luther launched the new Protestant Reformation. And the crackling flames of dissatisfaction quickly spread over all Europe in a storm of revolt against the power of the church. These protestors disclaimed the old church of their fathers. Throughout the land, righteous people determined to win liberation from the old doctrines and practices. They wanted to worship God, not the church. Equality in the sight of God was their claim. Direct communication with God was their desire. They helped God bring the world, step by step, closer to the ultimate goal.

Later in England, the people again protested against the intolerable corruption of the autocratic church. There was an outcry for the purification of the Church of England. The Puritan movement began, and it quickly spread even amid great persecution. These new seekers threatened the established church leaders, who used almost any means to suppress the new movement. Those who truly wanted the freedom of worship soon had either to flee or to be imprisoned. Their spirit was strong, but they had little power to resist and nowhere to turn. They fled to Holland. And still they longed for some new world, some new heaven and new earth where they could find freedom to worship God.

America must have seemed attractive to those who were dreaming of a new world. Even though America was unknown territory, it promised them the freedom of worship they craved. The Puritans felt a strong desire to create a community of their own. America seemed an ideal place, so they made the courageous decision to venture there. They committed themselves to the treacherous journey across the Atlantic. They risked their very lives, finding strength in their faith, which was stronger than life itself.

Think of it: They had to give up their families, their relatives, their surroundings, and their country, and head toward an unknown land. Their only hope was in God. Every step they took they depended upon God. Their journey was long, and there were many storms. They prayed unceasingly to God. They had but one way to turn. They turned to God. When they were sick and dying on the voyage, they had no medicine to take, no doctor to care for them; they turned to God. Those Pilgrim men and women were one with God. And that is how they survived.

Put yourself in their position of total reliance on God. What a wonderful faith! I am sure that the faith of the Pilgrim Fathers touched the heart of God. And when God is moved, He offers promises; and when He makes promises, He will fulfill them. God determined to give these faithful people the ultimate thing they wanted — freedom of worship. He then determined to give them even more.

I am sure you know, as I have learned, that the *Mayflower* arrived at Plymouth Rock in New England almost in the dead of winter. November in New England is rather cold. The destiny of the newcomers could have been only starvation because there was so little food to eat. Given this fact, it really inspired me to learn about the store of grain in the hold of the *Mayflower* which they would not touch, even though they were starving to death. They preserved this grain for planting the next spring. This was truly a supreme example of sacrifice. They preferred to die hoping in tomorrow, rather than to act in desperation for only a few more days of life.

The Pilgrims came to this land full of purpose and hope. They knew that this purpose of theirs was more important than preserving their own lives. Nothing could have given them this kind of courage, this kind of dedication, this kind of sacrificial spirit except their faith in God. When they arrived at Plymouth, the 41 men who had survived the voyage got together and organized their ideas for government. The resulting Mayflower Compact was signed, "In the Name of God, Amen." This is really a wonderful story. This little group of people left Europe with their hope set in God. They grew sick and died in God; they survived in God. They formed their first government and signed their official papers, "In the Name of God."

The story of the American Pilgrim Fathers is one of a kind in God's history. It fits into the pattern of the righteous people of history, such as Abraham, Isaac, and Moses. These Pilgrims were the Abrahams of modern history. They therefore had to brave many hardships even after the Mayflower Compact was signed.

During the first winter in America, the population of the hardy *Mayflower* survivors was cut in half. Each day that winter brought a heartbreaking separation from loved ones. One by one these courageous pioneers died. Yet their life from morning to night, from dusk to dawn, was centered upon the will of God. God was their only comfort, their only hope and their only security. God was the principal Partner for them. Here was an example of such a rare and pure group of God's people. They demonstrated untiring faith, and God gave them power and courage. They never lost their trust in God and their vision of the future. Their purpose in coming to America was to build a nation centered on God, to establish the land where God could dwell, where they could really share fellowship with each other and rejoice in fellowship with God. This was all in God's Providence, because He needed a nation to serve as His champion for the ultimate and permanent salvation of the world.

So another miracle came to the Pilgrims. When they were just barely surviving and their population had been halved, the Indians could easily have wiped them out with one stroke. But again, God was a shield for them. The first group of Indians the *Mayflower* survivors encountered were not hostile. The Indians welcomed the settlers. If the Pilgrims had been destroyed at that time, there would probably have been no America for God. God intervened to save His people here in America. This is my belief. God wanted them to settle, and He gave the Pilgrims a chance.

As the population of the settlement grew, they had to push the Indians away to enlarge their own colony. Of course, this land did not belong to the new American people originally. The Indians were the inhabitants of the land, and the Pilgrim settlers must have been invaders in the eyes of the Indians. Why then did God give these settlers their great chance? Here is my interpretation: God sided with the American settlers because it was in His plan. Furthermore, these American settlers met God's requirements and truly demonstrated an unwavering faith in God. God could not help but give them His promise and fulfill that promise.

America's existence was according to God's Providence. God needed to build one powerful Christian nation on earth for His future work. After all, America belonged to God first, and only after that to the Indians. This is the only interpretation that can justify the position of the Pilgrim settlers.

This continent of America was hidden away for a special purpose and was not discovered until the appropriate hour. The people of God came at the appointed hour. They came to mold the new way of life. Their principal Partner was God. At home, in caring for their children, in farming or cooking or building, they let God share their work. He was the only security they had. A farmer might talk to his son working out in the field with him, "Let's plow this field in the name of God." Their everyday life was lived in the name of God.

After the first spring visited them, they cleared the fields, planted, cultivated, and harvested the crop. And they attributed all their precious harvest to the grace of God. The beautiful tradition of Thanksgiving thus originated. Following the next severe winter, the first thing they built was a church. The first road they built was the road to the church. At night, at dawn, in the morning and at noontime, they prayed to God. I am sure they prayed, "God, we want to build a place for You which must be better than the Old World. We want to build a place where You can dwell and be master."

And they also had a vision of the future that this Christian nation would do more good for the rest of the world than any other country upon the face of the earth. I am sure that after their church they built a school. They wanted outstanding schools for their children, better than any schools existing in the Old World. And their homes came last. After they built these homes, they dedicated them to God. This is the history of your Pilgrim Fathers, I know. I can visualize early America as a beautiful America, because God was dwelling everywhere. In the school, in the church, in the kitchen, in the street — in any assembly or marketplace, God was dwelling.

I understand that in America you are approaching your nation's 200th birthday. Let us therefore examine the people who led the independence movement in this country in 1776. Those freedom fighters were traitors in the eyes of the British Crown. But God could use these traitors as His instruments, as His people, and through them He conceived and built the best nation upon the face of the earth.

George Washington, commander in chief of the Continental Army, tasted the bitterness of defeat in many, many battles. When he finally faced the last heartbreaking winter at Valley Forge, he was serious. I am sure George Washington prayed like this: "God, it is You who led our people out of Europe and brought us over here to the New World; You don't want us to repeat the dull, gray history of Europe. You liberated us and gave us freedom. You don't want to see the mistakes in Europe repeated in this land. Let me give you my pledge. I will build *one nation under God*." Thus George Washington made his battle God's battle, and therefore the victory won was a victory for God.

I know that this victory and the independence of America came because God accepted George Washington's prayer, along with the prayers of many other Americans. God knew that His champions would work for His new nation. But

George Washington had nothing to work with, and the British army had everything — power, authority, tradition, and equipment. They were proud of their military strength. The American Continental Army had no ammunition and few soldiers. George Washington had finally one weapon only: faith in God. I believe that George Washington's position paralleled David's in his fight against the giant Goliath. David won his battle in the name of God. George Washington won his battle in the name of God. They both let God vanquish their foe. Each of them put his whole heart, his whole being, his whole sacrificial spirit into the battle, and won.

Now it is a significant fact that throughout history, God's people could never be blessed on their own homeland. God moves them out of their homeland and settles them on foreign soil, and there they can become a people and a nation of God. According to the pattern, the American people journeyed in faith out of their homelands, came across the ocean to the New World, and here they received God's blessing. God had a definite plan for America. He needed to have this nation prosper as one nation under God. With God, nothing is impossible. So out of the realm of impossibility the independence of America became a fact, and upon its foundation, great prosperity came.

The British army fought for their king. For them, the British Crown was supreme. The American army fought for their King. God was their only King, and He alone was supreme. The New World was pioneered in the name of God. America is called "the land of opportunity." Here is the soil on which people find opportunity in God.

The Christian tradition in America is a most beautiful thing for foreigners to behold when they come to this country. I learned that every day your Congress is convened in prayer. Your President is sworn into office by putting his hand on the Bible. One day I visited a small prayer room in your Capitol building. When your leaders have grave decisions to make, they come to this place, kneel humbly before God and ask His help. There is a stained glass window depicting George Washington on his knees in prayer. Here I saw the true greatness of America. From the highest echelons of Congress, way down to the rustic customs of the countryside, evidence of dependence on God can be seen everywhere in America.

In this respect America is a unique nation. Even your money, the bills and coins, are impressed with such a beautiful inscription, "In God We Trust." No other nation does such a thing. Then whose money is it, your money? Is it American money? No, it is God's money. Every bill or coin says so. You are the stewards, and God has deposited His wealth in your hands. Yes, this nation is not the American nation, it is God's nation. And such a nation exists for the entire world, not just for America herself. Yes, America was formed as a new nation, a new Christian nation under a new tradition. The shackles of old traditions fell away in America. You must want to build a new nation under God.

God's purpose is the salvation of the world and all mankind. Today in America, therefore, you must not think that you have such wealth because you yourselves are great. We must humbly realize that the blessing of God came to America with the purpose of making it possible for God to use this nation as His instrument in saving the world. If America betrays God, where can God go? If America rejects God, where can God go to fulfill His aim? Do you want to let Him try to go to the communist world? To underdeveloped countries? God wants to have America as His base, America as

His champion. And America was begun in the sacrificial spirit pursuing God's purpose. America must consummate her history in the same sacrificial spirit for God's purpose. Then America will endure forever!

Let me compare two striking examples. The people who came to America—to North America—came seeking God and freedom of worship. The sole motive of the first settlers was God. When they came for God, they not only found God, but they also found freedom and wealth. At the same time, many people went to South America. Their sole motivation was to find gold. South America is a fertile land, no less than the North American continent. But when the colonists' motivation was gold, they could find neither gold, nor God, nor freedom. And the South American countries remain underdeveloped nations.

America is the miracle of modern history. You have built the most powerful nation in history in a short time. Was this miracle possible only because you worked hard? Certainly you did work hard. However, hard work is not explanation enough. If God had not been the principal Partner, creating today's America would have been impossible. God played a prime role in American history, and this He wants America to know.

The time has come for the American people to be awakened. Because of the noble beginning of this country, God sent His blessing and promise. The sacrificial devotion of your ancestors was the foundation for God's blessing. If you betray your ancestors, if you betray God, there is only one way for America to go. It will go to destruction. Since America was built on the pillars of faith in God, if God is moved out of American life, your nation will be without support. Your decline will be rapid.

We reap as we sow. Today the world is divided into two major camps and a global struggle faces us. Why has this phenomenon occurred? History was sown in the time of Jesus. Jesus was the seed of history. His crucifixion was the sowing. There were two thieves crucified with Jesus, one on the right-hand side, and one on the left-hand side.

Since Jesus went into heaven through the cross, at the time of reaping he will return through the cross. The circumstances at the time of the crucifixion of Jesus form the pattern which will be repeated on the global scale when the time of his return comes. And that time is now.

Today, we are aware that communism is a strong force in this world. The communists say, "There is no God." And the democratic world or free world says, "God exists." Why do we call the democratic faction in politics "right," and the communist faction "left"? Where did this terminology come from? There is an ultimate reason seen from the historical perspective we have been pursuing. This was already determined at the time of Jesus' crucifixion. The thief crucified on Jesus' right side foreshadowed the democratic world, and the thief crucified on Jesus' left side represented the communist world.

The thief on the left side condemned Jesus even on the cross, saying, "Are you not the Christ? Save yourself and us!" (Luke 23:39). He was saying: If you really were the Son of God, you would come down and save yourself and save me. Jesus was silent. He did not answer the man. There was also a defender of Jesus, the thief on the right. He said to the thief on the left, "Do you not fear God, since you are under the same sentence of condemnation? And we indeed justly; for we are receiving the due reward of our deeds; but this man has done nothing wrong" (Luke 23:40-41).

What faith was shown by this man on the right-hand side of the cross! He forgot his own death and defended Jesus. What a noble deed! And Jesus responded: "Truly, I say to you, today you will be with me in Paradise" (Luke 23:43).

At this moment the seed was sown by the left-hand side thief that the God-denying world would come into being— the communist world today. And the seed for the existence of a God-fearing world was sown by the thief on the right-hand side. The free world is in the position of the right-hand side thief. And America is the center of those God-fearing free world nations. America has been chosen as the defender of God, whereas communism says to the world, "There is no God."

It is America's position to say to the communists, "What are you talking about? God exists. God dwells right here, with us." Is America taking this position? No! Today's America is quickly turning self-centered and away from God. America doesn't seem to care about the rest of the world. But you must give America to the rest of the world as a champion for God. When America helped others, sent out missionaries and more aid to starving people, she enjoyed her golden age. Confrontation with communism could be done from a position of strength at that time.

But today America is retreating. It is not just an accident that great tragedy is constantly striking America and the world, such as the assassination of President Kennedy and the sudden death of Secretary-General Hammarskjold of the United Nations, both in the same decade. The spirit of America has declined since then. Unless this nation, unless the leadership of this nation, lives up to the mission ordained

51

by God, many troubles will plague you. God is beginning to leave America. This is God's warning.

In our time, all Christians should be world champions, destined to fulfill for God the role of the right-hand side thief. Christians must rise and be willing to struggle for the salvation of the world. But Christians today are too busy perfecting their separate denominations and church interests. We must unite with the coming of the Lord. The end of the world signifies that the time of the arrival of the Lord of the Second Advent is near. He must have a base somewhere, some foundation prepared upon which he can begin to fulfill his mission. America is meant to be that base, but America is deeply troubled.

When I first came to America, I went to New York and stood on Fifth Avenue during the rush hour. Suddenly tears began pouring down my face. I looked at the wonder of the Empire State Building and the magnificence of the new Trade Center—the tallest buildings in the world. But I asked myself, "Does God dwell in those buildings?"

New York is becoming more and more a city without God. It is a city of crime. Such a beautiful city is now crumbling. I can see so much immorality and so many signs of godlessness in that city. It was shocking to my eyes as I stood watching during that rush hour. I could see so many things at once that are all intolerable in the sight of God.

I asked God, "Is this the purpose for which You blessed America?" I know God wants to see His spirit prevail in those great buildings. In those beautiful automobiles He wants to see young people bubbling with enthusiasm for God and the love of others. It doesn't take the Empire State Building to glorify God; it doesn't take a 1973 automobile to glorify God. Even if you have only a rock as your altar, when you pour out your hope and your tears upon it for the service of God, God is with you. I can really see that God is leaving the great city of New York. New York is instead becoming the city of evil.

America has been known as the "melting pot" where people of all colors, creeds, and nationalities are melted into one new breed. In order to melt anything, heat is required. Do you know who provided the heat for America? God was that heat. Without God, you could never have melted your people together.

America could only achieve true brotherhood through the Christian spirit, but when you begin to lose this foundation, America's moral fiber will deteriorate. Today there are many signs of the decline of America. What about the American young people? What about your drug problems and your juvenile crime problems? What about the breakdown of your families? I hear that three out of every four marriages in America will end in divorce. The California state government is issuing more divorce certificates than marriage licenses.

What about racial problems and the threat of communism? And what about the economic crises? Why are all these problems occurring? These are all signs that God is leaving America. I can read the sign which says, "God is leaving America now!" If this trend continues, in a very short time God will be with you no longer. God is leaving America's homes. God is leaving your society. God is leaving your schools. God is leaving your churches. God is leaving America. There are many signs of atheism in this once God-centered nation: There have been many laws enacted that only a godless society could accept. There was a time when prayer was America's daily diet. Today you hear prayers in American schools no longer.

You may want to ask, "Who are you to say these things to the American people?" Then please raise your hands if any of you can take the responsibility for this country. For the last ten years American churches have been declining in spirit; American churches are becoming senior citizens' homes. The future of America depends upon the young people, and the churches are failing to inspire American youth. We need a spiritual revolution in America. A revolution of heart must come to America. Individualism must be tied into God-centered ideology. Who is going to do this? Who is going to kindle the hearts of American youth? Will the President do this? Will wealthy American businessmen do this? Will American churches do this?

I know that God sent me here to America. I did not come here for the luxurious life in America. Not at all! I came to America not for my own purposes, but because God sent me. For 6,000 years God has been working to build this nation. The future of the entire world hinges on America. God has a very great stake in America. Somebody must come to America and stop God from leaving.

My followers in Korea bade me farewell in tears. I know there are still many things to do in Korea. But working with only Korea would delay world salvation. America must be God's champion. I know clearly that the will of God is centered upon America. I came from Korea, I gave up my surroundings in Korea, just as many people have in the history of God's providence. I do not come to this country to make money. When I came to America, I committed my fortune, my family, and my entire life to America. I came to a new country where I can serve the will of God.

We must be humble. We must initiate from this moment the greatest movement ever on earth, the movement to bring God back home. All of your pride, your wealth, your cars and your great cities are like dust without God. We must bring God back home. In your homes, your churches, your schools and your national life, our work for God's purpose must begin. Let's bring God back, and make God's presence in America a living reality.

I have initiated a youth movement which is probably the only one of its kind in United States history. This is a new Pilgrim movement. Does it seem strange that a man from Korea is initiating an American youth movement for God? When you have a sick member of your family, a doctor comes from outside of your house. When your house is on fire, the firefighters come from outside. God has a strange way of fulfilling His purpose. If there is no one in America meeting your needs, there is no reason why someone from outside cannot fulfill that role. America belongs to those who love her most.

The mere numbers of the Christian population in America are not impressive. You cannot impress God with numbers, but only with fervent faith. The standard is the quality of Abraham's faith. How many Christians in America are really crying out with fervor for God? How many American Christians feel that God's work is their own work? How many people put God first? How many are ready to die for God?

Somebody must begin, and begin now. Even under persecution, somebody must begin. Someone must give himself up for the purpose of God and bring God back home. We must have our churches filled with fiery faith; we must create new homes where our families can be really happy, and we must finally create a new society, a new spiritual nation where God can dwell. America must go beyond America! This is the only way for this country to survive. I know this clearly: This is the will of God. Therefore, I have come to America, where I become one voice crying in the wilderness of the 20th century.

In the last few weeks, and in particular in the last few days, our Unification Church people greeted every one of you—and not just once, twice, or three times. You are almost tired of them, I am sure. But put yourself in these young people's positions. Why are they doing this? Does it bring them any material profit? Eighty-five percent of the young people in our movement are college graduates. They are capable of earning tens of thousands of dollars a year, but instead they are going out on the streets asking you to come to these lectures. Their hearts are compassionate. They have one purpose: They want to save America. They want to bring God back to America and they know that by serving the world they can save America.

These young people are here to rekindle America's spirit. America has a great tradition. All you have to do is revive it. We need a new movement of Pilgrims with a new vision. This is inevitable, because God left no alternative for America. You have no other direction to turn. The new Pilgrim movement has come—not for America alone, but for the world. In other words, the movement for world salvation must begin in this country. America is the base, and when America fulfills her mission you will be eternally blessed.

This is God's hope for America. This is God's ardent hope for you. For myself, I made a covenant with our young people of America that we will strive in partnership with

God for this great crusade. I want you to join, I want you to support these young people.

There is nowhere else to turn. When you bring God back into your home, your home will be secure. Your juvenile delinquency problem will be solved. There is no good answer to the racial problem except God. Communism will be no threat when God is made real. God will increase your wealth. This is the one way that America can save herself.

This is my deep desire, from my heart, that America will see the glorious day of renewal. And for this reason I come to speak to you with God's hope for America.

I really appreciate, particularly tonight, every one of you who comes and listens so thoughtfully. May God bless your home, bless your work. Thank you very much.

The Future of Christianity

Theatre for the Performing Arts,
New Orleans, Louisiana
October 28, 1973

Ladies and gentlemen, thank you very much for coming tonight. My topic this evening is, "The Future of Christianity."

Tonight I am going to speak about some new revelations from God which are very vital to the understanding of all Christians. I will also frequently mention the chosen people of Israel. I am sure there are many Christians and Jewish people in the audience. I dearly love all Christian brothers and sisters, and I have high esteem for the Jewish people. I beg you to understand before I begin that what I will say in no way reflects my personal feeling. I am only bearing witness to the truth.

Sometimes testimony to the truth is a painful task. Yet it is a mission it is my duty to fulfill. The content of my message tonight may be contrary to your previous understandings. Some things may be very new to you. I would like to ask that you think over seriously what you are about to hear.

Unless I had something new to reveal, I would not come here to speak to you at all. Why should I come only to repeat things that you already know? I would like for you and me to spend this time together in openmindedness so that the spirit of God can speak directly into our hearts. Jesus taught in his Sermon on the Mount:

> Blessed are the poor in spirit, for theirs is the kingdom of heaven.
> Blessed are the meek, for they shall inherit the earth.
> Blessed are those who hunger and thirst for righteousness, for they shall be satisfied. (Matt. 5:3,5-6)

Tonight I humbly ask you to be the poor in spirit; I ask you to be the meek, and I ask you to become those who hunger and thirst for righteousness. Then we will all see the Kingdom of Heaven, and we shall all be satisfied. Now let us begin.

Christians, and Christianity itself, have a final hill to cross. Biblical prophecy states that Christians must pass through the end of the world and face the judgment of fire at the great and terrible day of the Lord. The Bible says we are going to see many extraordinary phenomena, in heaven and on earth, as the end comes near.

When Jesus promised his Second Coming, he conveyed a feeling of great imminence. From the day Jesus Christ ascended into heaven, Christians have been watching for his return to earth. For the last 2,000 years of history, it has been the hope of every Christian to see the returning Christ. But this extraordinary event has never occurred. Many people are tired of waiting. Some finally decided that this Second Coming would not happen literally. They came to think, "This is just one of God's methods to keep us alert."

Tonight we must clarify the meaning of the end of the world as the Bible prophesies it. We must also know how the Lord will reappear when he comes in the fullness of time.

We should first of all understand that God did not create the world to end. He always intended the world of goodness to last forever. The God who does not create for eternity cannot be an almighty God. The present world must end, however, because the fall of man initiated a history of evil. The end of the world is necessary because we have not achieved God's intended world of goodness. Instead of becoming children of goodness, we have in reality become creatures of evil.

Adam and Eve fell in the Garden of Eden. They were not at that time in a position to have a clear understanding of the will of God. They entered into a state of confusion and made the wrong choice. They were confronted with either obedience to God, which would have brought about the good world, or obedience to Satan, which did in fact bring about their fall. Between two clear choices, Adam and Eve made the wrong one. They brought evil into the world. God's original intention was to create His ideal world — a good and prosperous world He determined to last for eternity. But man fell, the good world of God ended abruptly, and human history started in the wrong direction.

The history of mankind is therefore a history of evil. God sowed good seed, and He intended to harvest a good crop. But Satan stole His crop before it was ripened and reaped a harvest of evil. Human history is a crop of weeds.

Then what does the end of the world mean? Just what is going to end? Evil is going to end. God will put an end to all evil. Out of God's new beginning will come a new opportunity for man. And the goodness God intended in His original ideal can be made real.

In the Garden of Eden, man fell into evil instead of developing his goodness. Man was subjugated by Satan and became the child of sin. Therefore the Bible says, "You are of your father the devil" (John 8:44). If the fall of man had not occurred, then the true ruler would be God. But He is not today the King of this universe, because Satan is sitting upon God's throne. God has to remove all results of the fall of man before He can truly reign over the world.

Now I will give you clearly the definition of the end of the world. The end of the world is the moment in history when God ends evil and begins His new age. It is the time of the cross junction between the old history of evil and the new history of good.

In light of this definition, why does the Bible predict extraordinary heavenly phenomena as signs of the end of the world? Will the things predicted really occur? The Bible says:

Immediately after the tribulation of those days the sun will be darkened, and the moon will not give its light, and the stars will fall from heaven, and the power of the heavens will be shaken. (Matt. 24:29)

What does this mean? What are we to expect?

First of all, please rest assured that these things will not happen literally. God will not destroy anything in the universe. God often expressed His truth in symbols and parables, and these Biblical sayings will be accomplished symbolically. Secondly, God has no reason to destroy the universe. It is not the universe, but man who has committed sin. Only man deviated from the original plan of God's creation. Why should God destroy the animals, or the plants, or anything in creation which fulfilled His purpose as He intended? God would not destroy those innocent things.

The Bible therefore says, "A generation goes, and a generation comes, but the earth remains forever" (Eccles. 1:4). But in Revelation we read: "Then I saw a new heaven and a new earth; for the first heaven and the first earth had passed away" (Rev. 21:1). That new heaven and new earth refers to the coming of the new history of God, a time of new dominion. After you buy a house, won't you move in your family and possessions? Then you will say that you have a new home, and you are the new master of the house. In the same way, when men of God occupy this universe, it will become a new heaven and a new earth.

We know that when winter ends, spring begins. But can we say at precisely what point spring starts? Who can pinpoint the exact instant of transition? You cannot know because the passage from one season to another takes place imperceptibly, quietly. The end of winter is similar to the beginning of spring, so there is no discernible moment of transition.

At what moment does the old day end and a new day begin? Although the change occurs in darkness, there is no doubt that we do go from one day to the next. The change is unnoticeable at first, but it is also inevitable and irrevocable. Although three billion people live on earth, not one among them can point to the exact moment when the old day passes and the new day begins. So we understand that from the human point of view we cannot always know the precise moment things happen. But God knows when winter passes into spring, and God knows when night opens into day. And God can point to the transition into new history.

Our step into new history is like a glorious dawn emerging out of the blackest night. The crossing point between good and evil is not obvious. You will not notice it when it happens, but it will definitely take place, just as surely as the sun will rise tomorrow.

Then how can we know when the end is approaching? God will not hide this moment from man; He does not suddenly bring judgment on the world without warning. God will announce the coming of the great and terrible day through his prophets. Amos 3:7 says, "Surely the Lord God does nothing, without revealing his secrets to his servants the prophets." God chooses His instrument and through him God announces His plans. This has been the case throughout Bible history.

The person to be chosen as God's prophet must be one of the people living in our evil world. But he must be a man of faith who can demonstrate that he is worthy to be used by God. He must show absolute faith. To do this he must give up all worldly success and completely separate himself from this evil world. He must purify himself by cutting off all evil attachments. He will not be popular in the evil world. God is absolute good and therefore the exact opposite of evil. That is why evil always persecutes a man of God.

Noah was such a man chosen by God and scorned by the evil world. God instructed Noah to build a ship. He sent Noah to the heights of a mountain instead of down by the riverside or to the seashore. God's command was so ridiculous in the eyes of the evil world that many people laughed at Noah. He was ridiculed, not because people thought him a particularly funny man, but because he followed God's instructions so faithfully. The eyes of the world could not understand the way of God. In this manner, with such implausible instructions, God could test the faith of the man he had chosen as His champion. This is what happened in Noah's day.

And at the time of Abraham it was no different. God called Abraham, the son of an idol-maker, and commanded him, "Leave your home at once!" God does not allow for any compromise. God takes a position where evil can be totally denied. In no other way can good begin.

God has said He will start a new history in which no element of evil will remain. God demands complete response from man. Those who follow God's direction must begin from absolute denial of the evil world. That is why Jesus Christ taught: "He who finds his life will lose it, and he who loses his life for my sake will find it" (Matt. 10:39). He also said, "A man's foes will be those of his own household" (Matt. 10:36).

You may ask, what kind of message is this? This is God's way, to choose His own people and put them in a position where they will be rejected by evil. Otherwise His champion can do no good for God. From the point of view of God's standard, then, modern Christians have been having a very easy time. This is very strange, because there is no easy way indicated in Christian teaching. I wonder, how many Christians are really serious about following the path of God? God's demand is absolute. It allows for no middle ground.

Then how can we know clearly the path of God? Let us examine the history of God's providence. Today we are anticipating the end of the world. God has made previous attempts to end the world. For example, the time of Noah was a crossroads in history, when God wanted to bring an end to evil and begin the world of goodness. Noah was the central figure chosen in God's dispensation. To better understand Noah's mission and the meaning of the end of the world, we want to know more fully how the evil history began.

In the Garden of Eden, God gave Adam and Eve a commandment. That commandment was the word of God. Then Satan approached and enticed them with a lie. And that lie was the word of evil. Adam and Eve were in a position to choose between the two words: The truth was on one side, and a lie was on the other. They chose the lie.

Because this was the process of the fall of man, at the end of the world God will give mankind truth. The words of God will come through His prophet. When man accepts the words of God he will then pass from death to life, because truth brings life. Man has died in a lie, and in truth he will be reborn.

Therefore judgment comes by words. These words of God's judgment will be revealed by His chosen prophets. This is the process of the ending of the world. Those who obey and listen to the new word of truth shall have life. Those who deny the word will continue to live in death.

God chose Noah to declare the word. Noah's announcement was, "The flood is coming. The salvation is the ark." The people could have saved themselves by listening to Noah's words. However, the people treated Noah as if he were a crazy man, and they perished — because they opposed the word of God. According to the Bible, only the eight people of Noah's immediate family became passengers on the ark. Only these eight believed, and only these eight were saved.

God had said to Noah, "I have determined to make an end of all flesh; for the earth is filled with violence through them; behold, I will destroy them with the earth" (Gen. 6:13). Did this actually happen? We know the evil people perished, but was the physical world demolished in the process? No. This passage was not literally fulfilled, and God did not destroy the earth. God did eradicate the people and destroy the evil sovereignty, leaving only the good people of Noah's family. This was God's way of beginning to restore the original world of goodness through Noah.

If God had fully consummated His restoration at that time, then we would have heard no more about the end of the world. Once the perfect world of goodness is realized, another end of the world is not necessary. Nothing could then interfere with the eternal reign of God's perfect kingdom.

But the very fact that we anticipate the end of the world today is proof that God did not succeed at the time of Noah. What happened to Noah after the flood should be fully explained, but I cannot spend too much time on that subject tonight. To make a long story short, once again, sin crept into Noah's family through his son, Ham. God's flood judgment was thereby nullified, and evil human history continued until the time of Jesus Christ.

With the coming of Christ, God again attempted to end the world. Jesus came to start the new Kingdom of Heaven on earth. Thus, the first words Jesus spoke were, "Repent, for the kingdom of heaven is at hand." Indeed, the time of Jesus Christ's ministry was the end of the world. That great and terrible day was prophesied by Malachi, about 400 years before the birth of Jesus:

> For behold, the day comes, burning like an oven, when all the arrogant and all evil-doers will be stubble; the day that comes shall burn them up, says the Lord of hosts, so that it will leave them neither root nor branch. (Mal. 4:1)

Was the judgment of Jesus Christ done by literal fire? Did the day come at the time of Jesus when everything literally turned to ashes? No, we know it did not. Since all these things prophesied did not literally happen at that time, some people say that such prophecy must have been meant for the time of the Second Advent. But this cannot be the case.

John the Baptist came to the world as the last prophet; Jesus said: "All the prophets and the law prophesied until John" (Matt. 11:13). The coming of John the Baptist should have put an end to prophecy and the Mosaic Law. This is what Jesus said would happen. The purpose of all prophecy before Jesus was to prepare for his coming, and to indicate what was to be fulfilled up to the time of his coming. These prophecies are not for the time of the Lord of the Second Advent. God sent His son Jesus into the world, intending full and perfect salvation to be accomplished. The Second Coming was made necessary only because God's will was left unfulfilled at the time of the first coming.

Why, then, was the time of Jesus the end of the world? We already know the answer. It is because Jesus came to end evil sovereignty and bring forth God's sovereignty upon the earth. This was the end of the Old Testament Age and the beginning of the age of the New Testament. Jesus brought the words of new truth.

How did the people receive the gospel which he brought? Those who were most faithful accused Jesus and crucified him. They were prisoners of the letter of the Old Testament and could not perceive the presence of the spirit of God in the new truth. It is ironic that Jesus fell victim to the very prophecies that were to testify to him as the Son of God. By the letter of the Mosaic Law he was judged a criminal. Blindly the people nailed him to the cross.

At the time of Jesus many learned people, many leaders of churches, and many people prominent in society who were well-versed in the Law and the prophets, were waiting for a Messiah. How happy they would have been to have their Messiah recite the Old Testament exactly, syllable by syllable and word by word! But Jesus Christ did not come to repeat the Mosaic Law. He came to pronounce a new law of God. People missed the whole point. And Jesus was accused. The people said to him, "We stone you for no good work, but for blasphemy; because you, being a man, make yourself God" (John 10:33).

The Bible states: "And they reviled him [one of Jesus' disciples], saying, 'You are his disciple, but we are disciples of Moses. We know that God has spoken to Moses, but as for this man, we do not know where he comes from' " (John 9:28-29). This was the way they looked at Jesus. Those people who diligently obeyed the letter of the Mosaic Law disobeyed Jesus Christ. The most devout among them were the first ones to be judged by Jesus and thrown into unquenchable fire.

Now at this time I would like to clarify the meaning of "judgment by fire."

We read in the New Testament: "The heavens will be kindled and dissolved and the elements will melt with fire!" (II Peter 3:12). How can this fantastic prophecy come true? Will it happen literally? No. The statement has symbolic meaning. God would not destroy His ideal on earth, His stars and all creation without realizing His ideal on earth. If He did, then God would become the God of defeat. And who would be His conqueror? It would be Satan. This can never happen to God.

Even on our human level, once we determine to do something, we see it through to completion. How much more so will God almighty accomplish His will. When God speaks of judgment by fire in the Bible, He does not mean He will bring judgment by flames. The significant meaning is a symbolic one.

Let us now consider another Biblical passage which speaks of fire. Jesus proclaimed, "I came to cast fire upon the earth; and would that it were already kindled!" (Luke 12:49). Did Jesus throw literal, blazing fire about? Of course not.

The fire in the Bible is symbolic. It stands for the word of God. This is why James 3:6 states, "The tongue is a fire." The tongue speaks the word, and the word is from God. Jesus himself said, "He who rejects me and does not receive my saying has a judge. The word that I have spoken will be his judge on the last day" (John 12:48).

In contemporary society, the word of the court executes judgment. The word is the law. In this universe, God is in the position of judge. Jesus came as the attorney with authority to oppose Satan, the prosecutor of man. Satan accuses man with his words, but these are false charges. Jesus champions the cause of believers, and his standard is the word of truth. God pronounces the sentence: His love is the standard, and love is His word. There is no difference between the earthly court and the heavenly court, in that both conduct their trials by words, not by fire.

So the world will not be burned up by fire when it is judged. The Bible states, "The Lord Jesus will slay him [the evil one] with the breath of his mouth" (II Thess. 2:8). The word of God is the breath of his mouth. Jesus came to slay the wicked by the word of God, and "He shall smite the earth with the rod of his mouth, and with the breath of his lips he shall slay the wicked" (Is. 11:4). What, then, is the "rod of his mouth"? We take this symbol to mean his tongue —through which he speaks the word of God.

Let's resolve this point completely. Look to where Jesus was instructing the people: "Truly, truly, I say to you, he who hears my word and believes him who sent me, has eternal life; he does not come into judgment, but has passed from death to life" (John 5:24). Men pass from death to life by words of truth. God will not send you the Messiah to burn you up. He will not send you the Messiah to set your houses afire or destroy your society. But if we reject the word of God spoken by the Lord, we leave no choice but to be condemned by judgment. Here is the reason why.

In the beginning God created man and the universe by His word — logos. Man denied the word of God and fell. Spiritual death has reigned ever since. Through His salvation work, God has been recreating man. Man fell by disobedience to God's word, and man shall be recreated by obedience to the same word of God. The word of God is given by the Lord. Accepting the word brings life out of death. Such death is the hell in which we live. Thus the word of God is the judge, and it will bring upon you a far more profound effect than the hottest flames.

Now at this time we can examine another important point. What would have happened if the people of Israel had wholeheartedly accepted Jesus Christ? Imagine the nation of Israel united with Jesus. What would that have meant? First of all, Jesus would not have been killed. People would have glorified Jesus as the living Lord. They would have then marched to Rome with the living Christ as their commander in chief, and Rome would have surrendered to the Son of God in his own lifetime. But in the sad reality of history, it took four centuries for a band of Jesus' disciples to conquer Rome. Jesus never won the chosen people of Israel, and he never gained the support he needed from them. He came to erect the kingdom of God on earth, but instead he had to caution his disciples even to keep his identity a secret because people did not accept his legitimacy as the Messiah, and he therefore lacked the power to be the King of kings.

Today we have much to learn, and we must not believe blindly. We must know the hidden truth behind the Bible. Jesus was crucified, not by his own will, but by the will of others. The faithlessness of the chosen people of Israel killed Jesus Christ.

Right now I am making a bold declaration. Jesus did not come to die. Jesus Christ was murdered. Let me repeat: Jesus Christ was murdered, his crucifixion was not the will of God. Even the Roman governor Pilate wanted to release Jesus. He did not find any fault with Jesus. But Christ's own people rejected him and forced Pilate to release Barabbas instead. What a pity! What a tragedy!

This may be shocking and astounding news to you, but if you are only surprised, then you have missed my purpose. I am revealing these things because of my duty to bear witness to the truth.

It was the chief priests, the elders, the scribes, and the faithful—who shouted in Pilate's court, "Crucify him!" St. Paul said, "None of the rulers of this age understood this; for if they had, they would not have crucified the Lord of glory" (I Cor. 2:8).

The people living at the time of Jesus Christ made a terrible mistake. But do you think they were so much more ignorant and less aware than we are today? No, not at all. They learned the Old Testament word for word and memorized the Mosaic Law. Based on their understanding, Jesus did not meet the qualifications to be the Messiah.

The people were in a very difficult position. If they wanted to believe the new words of Jesus, they had to abandon their traditional understanding of the Mosaic Law. Four thousand years of tradition had been based on the Old Testament. It was very, very difficult for people to just wake up one morning, turn away from the Law, and totally accept Jesus Christ as the Son of God. Because people had their eyes riveted to the letter of the Law, the spirit of the Law simply passed them by.

Let us look into the Old Testament and examine the prophecy of Malachi: "I will send you Elijah the prophet before the great and terrible day of the Lord comes. And he will turn the hearts of fathers to their children and the hearts of children to their fathers" (Mal. 4:5-6). The people of Israel knew God's promise clearly. They knew it by heart. And they expected the coming of Elijah before the Messiah appeared. When the Messiah did come, naturally they asked, "Where is Elijah?"

Elijah had been a prophet who performed miraculous works about 900 years before Christ. And it was written he ascended into heaven in a chariot of fire. Since Elijah ascended upward into heaven, he was expected to return from heaven. Did such a miracle happen before the coming of Jesus? Did the people hear any news about the arrival of Elijah? No, they did not. But what they did hear one day was the voice of Jesus Christ declaring, "I am the Son of God, the only begotten Son of God." And Jesus spoke not timidly, but with authority and power. Such a man could not be ignored.

This presented a great dilemma for the people of Israel. They immediately asked, "If this Jesus is the Messiah, then where is Elijah?" They earnestly expected the Messiah at that time, so they were also waiting for Elijah. They believed he would come straight down from heaven, right out of the sky, and the Messiah would come soon after, in a similar manner.

So when Jesus proclaimed himself as the Son of God, the Jewish people became puzzled. If there had come no Elijah, then there could be no Messiah. And no one had told them that Elijah had come. The disciples of Jesus were also confused. When they went out to preach the gospel, people persistently denied that Jesus could be the Son of God because the disciples were unable to prove that Elijah had come. They confronted this problem everywhere they went.

The disciples of Jesus were not educated in the Old Testament. Many learned people rebuked them when they went out to preach, asking, "Do you not know the Old Testament? Do you not know the Mosaic Law?" The disciples were embarrassed when they were attacked through the verses of the Law and the prophets. One day they came back to Jesus and put the question to him:

> "Why do the scribes say that first Elijah must come?" And Jesus answered, "Elijah does come, and he is to restore all things; but I tell you that Elijah has already come, and they did not know him, but did to him whatever they pleased. So also the Son of man will suffer at their hands." Then the disciples understood that he was speaking to them of John the Baptist. (Matt. 17:10-13)

According to Jesus, John the Baptist was Elijah.

This was the truth. We have determined the truth according to the words of Jesus Christ. But the disciples of Jesus could not convince the elders and chief priests and scribes of this fact. To those men, the idea was simply ridiculous. The only authority that supported such a notion was the word of Jesus of Nazareth. That is why the testimony of John the Baptist was so crucial. But alas, John himself denied that he was Elijah when he was asked! His denial made Jesus look like a liar.

Read the Bible:

> And this is the testimony of John, when the Jews sent priests and Levites from Jerusalem to ask him, "Who are you?"... And they asked him, "What then? Are you Elijah?" He said, "I am not." "Are you the prophet?" And he answered, "No." (John 1:19-21)

John himself said, "I am not Elijah." But Jesus had said, "He is Elijah."

John made it almost impossible for the people to know that Elijah had come. But Jesus declared the truth anyway. He said, "If you are willing to accept it, he [John the Baptist] is Elijah who is to come" (Matt. 11:14). Jesus knew that most people could not accept the truth. Instead, they questioned the motivation of Jesus. In order for Jesus to seem like the Messiah, Elijah had to come first, so the people thought he was lying for the purpose of his own self-aggrandizement. The Son of God became more and more misunderstood by the people.

This was such a grave situation. In those days, the influence of John the Baptist was felt in every corner of Israel. But Jesus Christ was an obscure and ambiguous figure in his society. Nobody was in a position to take Jesus' words as the truth. This failure of John was the major cause of the crucifixion of Jesus.

John the Baptist had already seen the Spirit of God descending upon the head of Jesus Christ at the Jordan. At that time he testified:

> "I saw the Spirit descend as a dove from heaven, and it remained on him. I myself did not know him; but he who sent me to baptize with water said to me, 'He on whom you see the Spirit descend and remain, this is he who baptizes with the Holy Spirit.' And I have seen and have borne witness that this is the Son of God."
> (John 1:32-34)

Yes, John the Baptist bore witness, and he did the job that God intended for him to do at that time. But later on, doubts came to him, and he finally succumbed to the many rumors circulating about Jesus. One such rumor called Jesus fatherless, an illegitimate child. John the Baptist certainly heard that rumor, and he wondered how such a person could be the Son of God. Even though he had witnessed to Jesus, John later became suspicious and betrayed him. If John the Baptist had truly united with Jesus Christ, he could have moved his people to accept Jesus as the Messiah, for the power and influence of John was very great in those days.

I am telling you many unusual things, and you may ask by what authority I am speaking. It is the authority of the Bible, and with the authority of revelation. Let us read the Bible together, and see word by word how John the Baptist acted.

> Now when John heard in prison about the deeds of the Christ, he sent word by his disciples and said to him, "Are you he who is to come, or shall we look for another?" (Matt. 11:2-3)

This was long after he had testified to Jesus as the Son of God. How could he even ask, "Are you he who is to come as the Son of God?" after the testimony of the Spirit to him? Jesus was truly sorrowful. He felt anger. Jesus refused to answer John the Baptist with a straight yes or no. He replied instead, "Blessed is he who takes no offense at me." Let me paraphrase what Jesus meant: "John, I am sorry that you took offense at me. At one time you recognized me, but now you doubt me. I am sorry your faith has proved to be so weak."

After this incident, Jesus spoke about John to his own disciples. He put a rhetorical question to them:

> "What did you go out to the wilderness to behold? A reed shaken by the wind? Why then did you go out? To see a man clothed in soft raiment? Behold, those

who wear soft raiment are in kings' houses. Why then did you go out? To see a prophet? Yes, I tell you, and more than a prophet. This is he of whom it is written, 'Behold, I send my messenger before thy face, who shall prepare thy way before thee.'" (Matt. 11:7-10)

What Jesus was saying here was this: "John, you went out to the wilderness to see the person who was more than a prophet — the Messiah, the Son of God. You have seen everything but missed the vital point, the core of your mission. You indeed failed to recognize me and failed to live up to God's expectation. It is God who expects of you 'to make ready for the Lord a people prepared.' You have failed."

Jesus concluded: "Truly, I say to you, among those born of women there has risen no one greater than John the Baptist; yet he who is least in the kingdom of heaven is greater than he" (Matt. 11:11). Conventional Christian interpretations have never fully explained the meaning of this controversial verse.

The missions of prophets through the ages were to prepare for or testify to the Messiah. Prophets always testified from a distance of time. John the Baptist was the greatest among prophets because he was the prophet contemporary with the Messiah, the prophet who could bear witness, in person, to the living Christ. But John failed to recognize the Messiah. Even the least of the prophets then living in the spiritual world knew Jesus was the Son of God. That is why John, who was given the greatest mission, and failed, became less than the least.

Jesus said, "From the days of John the Baptist until now the kingdom of heaven has suffered violence, and men of violence take it by force" (Matt. 11:12). John the Baptist was the chosen instrument of God, destined to be the chief disciple of Jesus. He failed in his responsibility, and Simon Peter, by the strength and force of his faith, earned that central position for himself on his own merit. Other men stronger and more violent in faith than John the Baptist fought relentlessly with Jesus for the realization of God's kingdom on earth. The devout men who righteously followed John the Baptist could not become the twelve disciples and seventy apostles of Christ, as they were to have been. If John the Baptist had become the chief disciple of Jesus, those two together would have united all of Israel. But the truth is that John the Baptist did not follow the Son of God.

One day John's followers came to him and asked, "Rabbi, he who was with you beyond the Jordan, to whom you bore witness, here he is, baptizing, and all are going to him" (John 3:26). There was concern in their question: "Look at all the people going to Jesus. What about you?" John the Baptist replied, "He must increase, but I must decrease" (John 3:30).

Usually Christians interpret this passage as proof of John's humble personality. This is an incorrect understanding of the meaning of his words. If Jesus and John had been united, their destiny would be to rise or fall together. Then Jesus could not increase his reputation while John's own prestige diminished! The lessening of his own role was what John feared. John once stated that the Messiah was the one "whose sandals I am not worthy to carry" (Matt. 3:11). Yet he failed to follow Jesus even after he knew that Jesus was the Son of God. John the Baptist was a man without excuse. He should have followed Jesus.

God sent John as a forerunner to the Messiah. His mission was clearly defined, "To make ready for the Lord a people prepared" (Luke 1:17). But because of John's betrayal, Jesus Christ had no ground upon which to start his ministry. The people had not been prepared to receive Jesus. Therefore, he had to go out from his home and work all by himself, trying to create a foundation on which the people could believe in him. There can be no doubt that John the Baptist was a man of failure. He was directly responsible for the crucifixion of Jesus Christ.

You may again want to ask me, "With what authority do you say these things?" I spoke with Jesus Christ in the spirit world. And I also spoke with John the Baptist. This is my authority. If you cannot at this time determine that my words are the truth, you will surely discover that they are in the course of time. These are hidden truths presented to you as new revelations. You have heard me speak from the Bible. If you believe the Bible you must believe what I am saying.

We must therefore come to this solemn conclusion: The crucifixion of Jesus was a result of the faithlessness of the Jewish people. The major cause of their faithlessness was the betrayal of John. Thus we have learned that Jesus did not come to die on the cross. If Jesus had come to die, then he would not have offered that tragic and anguished prayer in the Garden of Gethsemane. Jesus said to his disciples:

> "My soul is very sorrowful, even to death; remain here, and watch with me." And going a little farther he fell on his face and prayed, "My Father, if it be possible, let this cup pass from me; nevertheless, not as I will, but as thou wilt." (Matt. 26:38-39)

Jesus prayed this way not just once, but three times. If death on the cross had been the fulfillment of God's will, Jesus would certainly have prayed instead, "Father, I am honored to die on the cross for Your will."

But Jesus prayed asking that this cup pass from him. If his prayer came out of his fear of death, such weakness would disqualify him as the Son of God. We have witnessed the courageous death of many martyrs throughout Christian history—and even elsewhere—people who not only overcame their fear of death, but made their final sacrifice a great victory. Out of so many martyrs, how could Jesus alone be the one to show his fear and weakness, particularly if his crucifixion was the glorious moment of his fulfillment of the will of God? Jesus did not pray this way from weakness. To believe such a thing is an outrage to Jesus Christ.

The prayer of Jesus in the Garden of Gethsemane did not come from his fear of death or suffering. Jesus would have been willing and ready to die a thousand times over if that could have achieved the will of God. He agonized right up to the moment of death, and he made one final plea to God, because he knew his death would only cause the prolongation of God's dispensation.

Jesus wanted to live and fulfill his mission. It is a tragic misunderstanding to believe that Jesus prayed for a little more earthly life out of the frailness of his human soul. Young Nathan Hale, in the American struggle for independence, was able to say at the time of his execution, "I regret that I have but one life to give for my country!" Do you think Jesus Christ was a lesser soul than Nathan Hale? No! Nathan Hale was a great patriot. But Jesus Christ is the Son of God.

Think this over. If Jesus came to die on the cross, would he not need a man to deliver him up? You know that Judas Iscariot is the disciple who betrayed Jesus. If Jesus fulfilled God's will with his death on the cross, then Judas should be glorified as the man who made the crucifixion possible. Judas would have been aiding God's dispensation. But Jesus said of Judas, "The Son of man goes as it is written of him, but woe to that man by whom the Son of man is betrayed! It would have been better for that man if he had not been born" (Matt. 26:24). Judas killed himself.

Furthermore, if God had wanted His son to be crucified, He did not need 4,000 years to prepare the chosen people. He would have done better to send Jesus to a tribe of barbarians, where he could have been killed even faster, and the will of God would have been realized more rapidly.

I must tell you again, it was the will of God to have Jesus Christ accepted by his people. That is why God labored in hope and anguish to prepare fertile soil for the heavenly seed of the Messiah. That is why God established His chosen people of Israel. That is why God sent prophet after prophet to awaken the people of Israel to ready themselves for the Lord.

God warned them and chastised them; He persuaded them and scolded them, because He wanted His people to accept His Son. One day the disciples asked Jesus, " 'What must we do, to be doing the works of God?' Jesus answered them, 'This is the work of God, that you believe in him whom he has sent' " (John 6:28-29). The chosen people of Israel did the very thing God had labored to prevent: They rejected the one He had sent.

Jesus had one purpose throughout the three years of his public ministry: acceptance. He could not fulfill his mission otherwise. From the very first day, he preached the gospel without equivocation, so that the people could hear the truth and accept him as the Son of God. The word of God should have led them to accept him. However, when Jesus saw that the people were not likely to receive him by the words of God alone, he began to perform mighty works. He hoped that people could recognize him through his miracles.

> Now Jesus did many other signs in the presence of the disciples, which are not written in this book; but these are written that you may believe that Jesus is the Christ, the Son of God, and that believing you may have life in his name. (John 20:30-31)

Jesus gave sight to the blind and made the lepers clean. He healed the lame and blessed the deaf with hearing. Jesus raised the dead. He did these things only because he wanted to be accepted. Yet the people said of him, "It is only by Beelzebul, the prince of demons, that this man casts out demons" (Matt. 12:24). What a heart-breaking situation! Jesus soon saw the hopelessness of gaining the acceptance of the people. In anger and desperation he chastised them: "You brood of vipers!" (Matt. 12:34). He did not hide his wrath, but exploded in anger. "Woe to you, Chorazin! woe to you, Bethsaida! for if the mighty works done in you had been done in Tyre and Sidon, they would have repented long ago in sackcloth and ashes" (Matt. 11:21). And he wept when he drew near the city of Jerusalem.

> O Jerusalem, Jerusalem, killing the prophets and stoning those who are sent to you! How often would I have gathered your children together as a hen gathers her brood under her wings, and you would not! (Matt. 23:37)

Who has ever understood this broken-hearted Jesus? He said, "Would that even today you knew the things that make for peace! But now they are hid from your eyes" (Luke

19:42). By that time Jesus knew that there was absolutely no hope of avoiding death. Yet he pleaded with God in Gethsemane, and he pleaded with God on the cross: "My God, my God, why hast thou forsaken me?" (Matt. 27:46).

Thus Jesus died on the cross, not of his own will, not of the will of God, but by the will of men. Christ was destined to return from that moment on. He will return to consummate his mission on earth. Mankind must await his second coming for the complete salvation of the world.

Many people may now ask, "What about the prophecies in the Old Testament concerning the death of Jesus on the cross?" I am aware of those prophecies, such as Isaiah, Chapter 53. We must know that there are dual lines of prophecy in the Bible. One group prophesies Jesus' rejection and death; the others, such as Isaiah, Chapters 9, 11, and 60, prophesy the glorious ministry of Jesus when the people accepted him as the Son of God, as the King of kings. For example:

> For to us a child is born, to us a son is given; and the government will be upon his shoulder, and his name will be called "Wonderful Counselor, Mighty God, Everlasting Father, Prince of Peace." Of the increase of his government and of peace there will be no end, upon the throne of David, and over his kingdom, to establish it, and to uphold it with justice and with righteousness from this time forth and forevermore. (Is. 9:6-7)

This is the prophecy of the Lord of Glory, Jesus as the King of Kings, and the Prince of Peace. On the other hand, we can read:

> Surely he has borne our griefs and carried our sorrows; yet we esteemed him stricken, smitten by God, and

afflicted. But he was wounded for our transgressions, he was bruised for our iniquities; upon him was the chastisement that made us whole, and with his stripes we are healed. (Is. 53:4-5)

This is the prophecy of the suffering Christ. It is indeed the prophecy of the crucifixion.

Then, once again, why did God prophesy in two contradictory ways in the Bible?

It is because God has to deal with men — fallen men — in His dispensation. And fallen man is wicked and untrustworthy and possesses the capacity of betrayal.

In a way God fears man, and Satan fears man also — because of man's ability to betray. God is absolute good, and He never changes His position; Satan is absolute evil, and he never changes his position either. In this respect God and Satan are similar. However, man is a mixture of good and evil. Man stands between God and Satan and has the ability to change. Therefore, man is unpredictable. One day a man may profess his untiring faith in God and desire to serve Him; and the next day the same man may curse God, unite with Satan and become his slave.

Since God did not know how man would respond to His providence for the Messiah, He had no choice but to predict two contradictory results — dual prophecies, each possible depending on man's actions. Thus, the faith of man was the factor determining which one of the two prophecies would be fulfilled.

In the case of Jesus, if the chosen people of Israel demonstrated faith and united with him, then he would be accepted. The full realization of the prophecy of the Lord of Glory would result.

On the other hand, if the people were faithless and rejected the Messiah when he came, inevitably the second prophecy, that of the suffering Christ, would be fulfilled. And history shows that the chosen people took the second way. Therefore, the prophecy of the suffering Lord became reality instead of the prophecy of the Lord of Glory. Thus the crucifixion and the story of the suffering Christ became the course of history.

Since the prophecy of the suffering Christ became fact in the time of Jesus, the prophecy of the Lord of Glory has been left unfulfilled. And this is the prophecy which will be fulfilled at the time of the Lord of the Second Advent.

I would like to also observe that the Bible does not provide much record of the life of Jesus prior to his public ministry, except for the story of his birth and a few accounts of his childhood. Haven't you ever wondered why?

For thirty years Jesus lived in great rejection and humiliation. There were many events and circumstances which grieved and agonized Jesus. He was a truly misunderstood person—in his society and even among his own family. Nobody, absolutely nobody treated him as the Son of God. He was not even accorded the common respect due to any man. His society ridiculed him. God's heart was very deeply grieved by Jesus' life. If I revealed just a glimpse of some of the situations of heartbreak and sorrow surrounding the manhood of Jesus, that obscure figure, the man of Nazareth, you would not only be shocked and stunned, but you would burst into tears of sorrow.

God did not wish mankind to know the tragedy, the heart-breaking reality of the humiliation of Jesus Christ. The death of Jesus was neither his will nor his fault. The death of Jesus was murder, and his body was taken by Satan. Our salvation in Christianity comes not from the cross but from the resurrection. Without the resurrection, Christianity has no power. The crucifixion itself was a criminal act of faithlessness. However, the resurrected Jesus brought new hope, new forgiveness, and a new power of salvation. Therefore, when we place our faith in Jesus Christ of resurrection and unite with him, our salvation comes.

Please ask seriously in your prayers for a final answer on these matters. Ask either Jesus Christ or God Himself. If Jesus had lived and fulfilled his primary mission of bringing the kingdom of God on earth, Christianity would never have been what it is today. The purpose of Jesus' coming was for the salvation of the world. The Jewish people were to be God's instruments. However, salvation was not intended only for God's chosen people. For every soul upon the face of the earth, Jesus is the savior. He is the savior of all mankind. Since Jesus left his mission uncompleted, he also left us the promise of his Second Coming.

Then let us examine when the end of the world will come. This is very important to us. The gospel says that in the last days God will separate the sheep from the goats. What is the difference between these two kinds of animals? Sheep recognize their master, the shepherd, while goats do not follow a shepherd. Today you know that our world is divided into two opposing camps. One is the democratic world, the other is the communist world. Our free world says, "There is a God." We accept our shepherd. The communist world says, "God does not exist." They deny their master. Thus the free world may be symbolized by sheep, and the communist world by goats. At the time of the formation of these two conflicting ideological worlds, we can know we have come to the end of the world.

How will the Lord of the Second Advent come? Our position as Christians exactly parallels the position of the elders, scribes and priests at the time of Jesus. In those days, the people were waiting for Elijah and the Messiah to arrive on the clouds of heaven. Why did the people think this way? Why did they hold this kind of belief?

They were simply following the Bible prophecy written down in Daniel 7:13: "I saw in the night visions, and behold, with the clouds of heaven there came one like a son of man, and he came to the Ancient of Days and was presented before him." Because of the great prophet Daniel, the people of Israel had every reason to expect the arrival of the Messiah with the clouds of heaven.

John said, "Many deceivers have gone out into the world, men who will not acknowledge the coming of Jesus Christ in the flesh; such a one is the deceiver and the antichrist" (II John 7). The Bible says that many people were denying the appearance of Jesus Christ in the flesh. And John condemned those people as the antichrist. But let us not forget the Old Testament prophecy of the coming of the Son of God on the clouds of heaven. Unless we know the whole truth, we, like the people of Jesus' time, will become victims of the literal words of the Bible.

Then, may I ask, what would you do if the Lord returned to earth not in the clouds but as a man in the flesh? What would you do? I am telling you, the Lord of the Second Advent will in fact appear as a son of man with flesh and bones. The first thing you may want to say is, "Rev. Moon, you are a heretic."

It is important to know on which side God will be and how God fulfills His plan. It is not important whether a man or his views are considered heretical or not. It does not matter how I look at the world or how you look at the world. It only matters how God looks at the world. And in God's view, we once again find in the Bible a dual prophecy concerning the coming of the Lord of the Second Advent. Revelation 1:7 definitely prophesies the arrival of the Lord of the Second Advent with the clouds. However, I Thessalonians 5:2 states: "For you yourselves know well that the day of the Lord will come like a thief in the night." There are then two opposing prophecies. What shall we do? Would you simply choose the prophecy which is most convenient for you?

Perhaps the Lord will appear with a loud noise on the clouds of heaven, because prophecy says so. But on the other hand, the Lord may appear like a thief in the night. If he comes on the clouds, he surely cannot slip into the world unseen like a thief. Tremendous attention would surround the spectacle of his coming on the clouds. I cannot imagine how such a thing could be hidden from your eyes.

Then just what is the truth? We have a crucial question before us. What is the truth? When you see the signs of the Last Days, the Bible urges you to go into a dark room and pray. Who can tell you the time of the Last Days? The angels do not know that day. Jesus said not even the Son of man knew when that day would arrive. Only God knows the time of the Last Days. That is why we have our answer from God. I am not saying you must believe me—not at all. I am just revealing what I know to be the truth, but you must verify this truth with God.

In the Last Days, the Bible says, do not just believe anybody. Do not believe me, and do not believe your church elders. Do not believe your ministers, and do not believe famous evangelists. Heaven is so near, and you can be lifted up by the spirit so high, that you can speak with God and receive the answer directly from Him if you are earnest enough.

There are many ministers in New Orleans, many clergymen and many church elders. How many of them are really listening for the voice of God? These ears of ours do not mean much, nor these eyes serve any useful purpose, unless we have spiritual ears and spiritual eyes. Jesus said, "He who has ears to hear, let him hear" (Matt. 11:15). And he said to his disciples, "But blessed are your eyes, for they see, and your ears, for they hear" (Matt. 13:16). He was not referring to the physical sense organs.

When you use your spiritual senses and listen for the word of God, you will find His direction and guidance. But it is not easy to become a citizen of the Kingdom of Heaven. It is very difficult for a foreigner simply to become a citizen of the United States. How much more difficult it is to remove ourselves from our earthly life and transfer ourselves into the Kingdom of Heaven. But we can achieve this very thing.

We know that even after Adam and Eve fell in the Garden of Eden, they were still able to communicate directly with God. Do you think that after the days of the Old and New Testaments, God has for some reason become deaf and dumb? No, God is very much alive, and today we can talk directly to Him. God can speak to you, and you can have a direct confrontation with Him.

The book of Acts of the Apostles says that in the Last Days, "Your sons and your daughters shall prophesy, and your young men shall see visions, and your old men shall dream dreams" (Acts 2:17). We must know the truth. We have to know how to apply for citizenship into the kingdom of God. We have to know when the Lord will come and how he will arrive.

Even with clear guidance in our lives, there is still the chance of failure to reach the goal. But today we have no guidance and no direction that we feel confident to follow.

Let us look to our Bible and clarify how the Lord of the Second Advent will appear. In Luke 17:20-22, Jesus was asked by the Pharisees how the kingdom of God was coming. He answered, "The kingdom of God is not coming with signs to be observed;...the kingdom of God is in the midst of you." Jesus then told his disciples, "The days are coming when you will desire to see one of the days of the Son of man, and you will not see it." But if the Lord comes on the clouds of heaven, how could we not see it? Revelation 1:7 says, "Every eye will see him, every one who pierced him."

What can this mean? Why would we not see him? The only way we might miss that day is if we look for the Lord to come from one direction, and he appears from another direction in an entirely unexpected manner, just as Elijah did at the time of Jesus. This is the reason you may not see the Lord at the time of his Second Coming.

Another mysterious prediction was given by Jesus Christ himself. He declared about the Lord at the Second Coming: "But first he must suffer many things and be rejected by this generation" (Luke 17:25). If Christ at his Second Coming appears in the glory of the clouds of heaven, who would dare deny him? Nobody would cause him suffering and pain.

The only way this prophecy can be fulfilled is if people expect his return on the clouds, and he suddenly appears as a humble man in the flesh. Do you not think that Christian leaders of today would make the same mistake that the priests and scribes and elders committed at the time of Jesus? Yes! They may very well deny him and reject him, because the manner of his coming would be very difficult for Christian leaders to accept. However, in this way the Bible will be fulfilled: He will first suffer and be rejected by this generation.

Jesus once asked a most important question: "When the Son of man comes, will he find faith on earth?" (Luke 18:8). How does this question concern us today, when Christian faith covers the face of the earth? It is because although we do have faith today, it may be mistaken faith—a belief which expects the Lord must come on the clouds of heaven. There are few men on earth with the kind of faith ready to accept the Son of man even appearing in the flesh. If this were not the situation, the Bible would not be fulfilled. Please note that Jesus did not say there would be no *believers,* but he said there would be no *faith.*

Jesus also said,

> Not every one who says to me, "Lord, lord," shall enter the kingdom of heaven, but he who does the will of my Father who is in heaven. On that day many will say to me, "Lord, lord, did we not prophesy in your name, and cast out demons in your name, and do many mighty works in your name?" And then will I declare to them, "I never knew you; depart from me, you evildoers." (Matt. 7:21-23)

This prophecy cannot be realized if his Second Coming is on the clouds of heaven.

At the time of the Second Advent, people will be again crying out, "Lord, Lord." At the same time they may be in the process of trying to crucify the Lord of the Second Advent himself if he appears in a manner different from their own expectations. They will then be the worst evildoers.

This is the Bible. Those who truly have eyes will see. Those who truly have ears will hear. Throughout history, God has sent His prophets before the time of fulfillment. He warns the people of His plan. No matter how devout Christian faith is today, no matter how many millions of people are in the Christian churches, they and their churches and their world will be doomed to decline once they fail to accept the Lord, however he may appear. This was the tragic fate of the people of Israel when they denied Jesus Christ, regardless of their righteousness otherwise.

We must therefore also be open to a new message. Jesus Christ did not come to repeat the Mosaic Law. Just as Jesus revealed himself with the new truth, the Lord of the Second Advent will reveal himself with God's new truth for our time. That truth will not simply be a repetition of the New Testament.

The Lord will not appear miraculously on the clouds of heaven. Why? Because God is sending His Son to restore the things that once were lost on earth. The first ancestors lost the kingdom of God on earth. Satan invaded the world and took Eve to his side, and then Eve took Adam away, leaving God alone and separated from man. All mankind has therefore suffered under the bondage of evil. God must send a new ancestor for humanity to begin a new history.

The work of God is restoration, always in the opposite direction from His original loss. This means that God first needs to find His perfected Adam, an Adam who instead of betraying God will become one with God. And then Adam must restore his bride in the position of Eve. Perfected Adam and perfected Eve, united together, will be able to overcome Satan and expel him from the world. In this way, the first righteous ancestors of humankind will begin a new history.

God's first beginning was alpha. This was invaded by evil, so He will restore the world in omega. Jesus is referred to as the second Adam in I Corinthians 15:45. God wanted to bless Adam and Eve in marriage when they were perfected. As a heavenly couple, they could bear children of God. This life was not realized in the Garden of Eden. That is why Jesus came in the position of Adam. God intended to find the true bride and have Jesus marry. The True Parents of mankind would have begun in the time of Jesus, and they could have overcome and changed the evil history of the world. Since that hope was not fulfilled by Jesus, after 2,000 years he is returning to earth as a man to complete in full the mission he only partially accomplished. The Kingdom of Heaven on earth will be established at that time.

The new history of goodness will thus begin. With the truth of God and True Parents for mankind, a new alpha in God's history will begin and continue for eternity. The ideal of God is to restore the first God-centered family on earth.

With this one model as a center, all the rest of mankind can be adopted into his family. We will become like them, and the first heavenly family will be expanded, multiplying into the tribal, national, and worldwide kingdom of God on earth.

The Kingdom of Heaven is to be literal and tangible. Jesus gave Peter the keys of the Kingdom of Heaven and said, "Whatever you bind on earth shall be bound in heaven, and whatever you loose on earth shall be loosed in heaven" (Matt. 16:19). So accomplishment on earth must precede fulfillment in heaven; the Kingdom of Heaven will be first achieved on earth.

At this time only an intermediate place in the spirit world is open. That is called "Paradise." Jesus and his disciples dwell in Paradise, and even they cannot actually enter the Kingdom of Heaven until it is established on earth. One reason for this is because the Kingdom of Heaven is prepared not for individuals, but for the family of God—for the father, the mother, and God's true children.

Ladies and gentlemen, I believe my message is absolutely clear and simple. God intended to begin the history of goodness in Adam. But Adam fell. God worked to restore history and begin anew in Jesus Christ. But the people of his time lacked faith and did not give him a chance. Therefore, the promise of the Lord of the Second Advent will be fulfilled. He is destined to come to earth as the Son of man in the flesh. He comes as the third Adam. He will take a bride and thereby bring about the most joyful day of heavenly matrimony, referred to as "the marriage supper of the Lamb" in the book of Revelation. He will fulfill the role of True Parents. True ancestry from God will be established, and heaven on earth can then be literally achieved.

We cannot doubt that Christianity today is in a definite crisis. This is a crisis parallel to the time of Jesus, when the established religious institutions failed the Son of God. We recognize this crisis of our time; but we can also see through the haze to the brightly shining day of new hope.

The end of the world is at hand, not only for Christians but for all people throughout the world. The new history of God will begin with the arrival of the Lord. Blessed are those who see him and accept him. It is the hope of Christianity to recognize, receive, and accept the Lord of the Second Advent. The chance has arrived for all of us. The greatest opportunity in any man's lifetime is now knocking at our door. Please be humble, and open yourselves to great new hope!

This is the time for unprecedented spiritual awakening. I want you to open your eyes and ears to perceive the truth. This is my hope, that by sharing this message with you, we might unite to prepare for the glorious day of the arrival of the Lord. Let us see the God of history, let us understand the God of Providence, and let us embrace the living God in our own lives.

Today is my last day in this city. I hope you will investigate these matters thoroughly. There is opportunity in New Orleans to come to our church and study or attend our workshops and explore the truth of the *Divine Principle*. I would not have come here if I did not bring with me new things to tell you. I am revealing new truth. This alone should be a compelling reason for you to look into the depths of this message.

I hope that, as I said in the beginning of our evening together, you will consider these ideas seriously and pray to God. He will answer you.

Thank you very much.

God's Way
of Life

1974 Day of Hope Banquet
Waldorf Astoria, New York City
September 17, 1974

Distinguished guests, ladies and gentle-
men, I am very happy to be here tonight. Thank you very
much for coming.

All people have certain characteristics in common. We
enjoy seeing beautiful things. We enjoy hearing beautiful
music, and, of course, we always enjoy good food. While we
were having this delicious dinner tonight, an outstanding
orchestra entertained us beautifully. So may I invite you to
join with me in giving them a warm round of applause?

First of all, I owe you an apology. As you were coming
into this banquet tonight, Mrs. Moon and I wanted to greet
you and shake hands with each one of you to express our
heartfelt welcome. But my staff advised against having a
receiving line, for if we were to shake hands with all of the
more than 1,700 guests, no time would be left for the ban-

97

quet. I regret not being able to meet each one of you personally. So to compensate for that, may I now shake hands with one gentleman and one lady among you as representatives of all guests tonight? [Rev. Moon shook hands with one man and woman in the front row.]

Secondly, I owe you another apology. During the last several weeks, hundreds of energetic young people from all over the world have been working in your city of New York. And this already noisy city of New York was made even noisier—all in the name of God, of course.

I am the one responsible for that. Furthermore, there have been many posters, and newspaper, TV, and radio ads announcing my meeting at Madison Square Garden tomorrow night. So I am sure that in this city by now almost everyone must be asking, "By the way, who *is* that Rev. Moon? Is he running for senator, or something?" That question is well answered tonight: Here I am, Rev. Moon. But I am not running for senator.

New York is a city of wonder. There is no end to unusual things in this city. When I first came to New York and observed the rush hour crowd on Fifth Avenue, I discovered a strange fact. I saw that all the people were walking with their heads down. So I thought that New Yorkers must be very humble, meek, and saintly, showing their inner respect to Almighty God by keeping their heads bowed even during the busy rush hour.

Months later, however, I found a more practical reason why New Yorkers walk with their heads down. As you know, New York is a city of skyscrapers. Millions of tourists come here to see them every day of the year. Those tourists walk around with their heads up, looking in awe at the Empire State Building and other great skyscrapers. Unless you watch out, your toes will be stepped on by those fascinated tourists, and your fashionable Madison Avenue shoes will look miserable by the end of the day. So New Yorkers, who are well accustomed to those majestic buildings, must look down and watch out to keep from getting stepped on.

But then I thought that the first and second reasons why New Yorkers have their heads down should be equally true. What the city of New York needs most today is God. And in order to have God, people must have humble and meek hearts. Only when we have a reverent attitude can God come into our hearts and into the city of New York. Let us make God real in New York, so that even during the rush hour on Fifth Avenue His presence will be so strongly felt that we cannot but bow our heads in thanksgiving and gratitude.

I love each one of you deeply and dearly, because I know God loves America and the American people — and I love God. Long before the birth of this nation, God was already preparing the North American continent, quietly setting it aside for His special dispensation.

In His divine will, at His appointed hour, God has raised up one great nation upon this blessed land — the United States of America. In such a short time, within only 200 years, God and the American people together have brought forth one of the most miraculous achievements in history.

This miracle is great evidence that God's abundant love has been poured out upon this great land of America. And God, who loves America, must especially love this city of New York, because New York is the greatest city in America.

This gathering here tonight represents the distinguished citizens of this great city of New York. Therefore God—who loves America and loves your city of New York—must love each one of you deeply and dearly. So I think God must be present with us here tonight.

I am really overwhelmed to be welcomed by this great and distinguished gathering in New York, in this beautiful setting. I am deeply honored to meet you here. My gratitude goes out to you, and I am truly thankful that you all came. What makes our meeting here unique is not that we are meeting in the grand setting of the Waldorf Astoria, but because we are here in the name of God. In a very real sense, God is our host tonight.

If I were to end my greeting to you at this point, then actually you still would not know very much about Rev. Moon. I am sure that you have come here to see me and hear me. And I would also like to leave you with a clear impression.

Therefore, if you would permit me, in the next few minutes I would like to leave you with a few grains of thought as a memory of my visit to your great city. Would you permit me to do so?

What is the most precious thing in your life? No doubt, the most precious things for you are happiness, joy, freedom, peace, and your ideals. This is common to all human beings. Therefore, throughout history, all people, regardless of their race or time, have sought true happiness, joy, freedom, peace, and certain ideals.

Also, all of us have an innate desire to have these precious things last for eternity, be unchanging and absolute. Because man has set his goals and ideals so high, he seldom attains them easily in the reality of life here on earth. Our world is always changing, and each man's stay here on earth is brief. Many have sought happiness, joy, freedom, peace, and their ideals, but very few have found them.

Having searched for eternal happiness in vain, we have to arrive at the conclusion that to find what is eternal, unchanging, and absolute, we must seek those things from an eternal and unchanging and absolute source. How can we find such a source? Is there such a source? Yes! It can only be Almighty God.

God is the Source of life. Not only that, God is also the Source of happiness and joy, the Source of freedom and peace, and indeed the Source of love and all ideals.

It may surprise you, however, to hear that to have these precious things is God's desire, too. God is seeking happiness, joy, love, and His ideal to be fulfilled for Himself also. However, as long as God is alone, He cannot experience these things. They remain dormant within Him.

The fulfillment of these goals can only be realized when a subject finds an object, and they unite in a reciprocal relationship of give and take, stimulating and complementing each other. Under that condition alone can these noble goals be attained.

The words "love" and "ideal" are without meaning when one is alone. Love requires someone to love and someone to be loved by. Hope or any ideal needs to be shared with someone. Love and ideals have meaning only when a reciprocal and complementary relationship of give and take has been established.

You may try to be happy by yourself, try to be joyful, try to be loving. But you can never attain these things when you are alone.

This is a universal truth. It even applies to Almighty God. As long as God remains alone, even He cannot fulfill these goals by Himself. Even Almighty God Himself needs someone to be in the position of an object to Him, someone to love and to be loved by.

For that reason, God created man as an *object to God*. God wanted to establish the reciprocal relationship of give and take with man so that He could be constantly stimulated in love and joy by that relationship. Have you ever thought that even God is helpless without *you*? Have you ever thought you are that precious and important in the sight of God?

Tonight I have had the pleasure of meeting many distinguished couples, husbands and wives. Let me ask you a question. Some years ago, when you were looking for your ideal mate, what was your standard? Did you want to have somebody who was *better or superior* to yourself, or somebody who was *inferior* to yourself?

You don't have to answer. The answer is obvious! Everyone is seeking someone better than himself or herself, because we all want to be associated with someone most ideal, someone perfect. We all know we may have some failings, some imperfections. But human desire always reaches for the highest. We all seek to have our dreams realized in our life partners.

Furthermore, as parents, do you want your children to be inferior to yourself, or would you want them to be superior to you? A father or mother would want unconditionally for their children to be better than themselves.

The other day, I saw a newborn baby. The parents of the baby are a very good-looking couple, yet the baby was not too handsome. She almost looked like an Idaho potato. But I said to that young couple, "Well, your baby is more beautiful and more handsome than her mommy and daddy!" Do you think that mommy and daddy were mad at me? No!

On the contrary, they said, "Thank you," and they beamed from ear to ear.

Why do we have traits and desires that work like this? All of our human characteristics come from one origin. We are the reflection of God. We act like we do because God acts that way. Our minds work the way they do because God's mind works that way. That's the way God is! That's the way we are. *We are like God, and God is like us.*

When Almighty God created man as His object, He wanted to have the very best. Just like any parent, God wants the very best for His children. *He wants His children to be even better than Himself.* The Heavenly Father wants His sons and daughters to be even better than Himself.

Yet man has not really known this most simple but profound truth. We did not realize that God is our Father and that He truly has parental love for us. He wants his children to be even better than Himself. We are that important, that precious to God. This is the ultimate value of man's life—that we are God's sons and daughters. And we have never understood that!

Since God is the eternal God, unchanging and absolute, when He created man He wanted man, His object, to be eternal, like Himself. He wanted man, His object, to be unchanging, like Himself. He wanted man, as His object, to be as unique and absolute as Himself.

So when we come to the realization that God is of this nature, then we realize that there can be no question about eternal life. The eternal life of man is more than real. Since God is eternal, He intends for His object to have eternal life, also. That is the logical conclusion.

By now, we know why God created man. We know that God is the Subject and we are His objects. Whenever there is a subject and object, there is the possibility of two different kinds of relationships between the two. One is a selfish relationship, where one dominates the other for the benefit of himself. The other is an unselfish relationship, where one gives himself wholeheartedly for the benefit of the other.

So when we think of these two kinds of relationships, which one would be God's choice? God knows that a selfish relationship is self-destructive. Nothing can flourish based on selfishness. Selfishness eventually leads to self-extinction. God knows that an eternal and prospering relationship can never come about through selfish taking. So God's choice was to have an unselfish relationship. He built the universe upon the base of unselfishness.

I see here in this audience many very prosperous and distinguished-looking gentlemen. We all generally have some pride and some ego. And I'm sure that every one of you has a certain pride in your own accomplishments. However, I want all you men to know that God, when He created man, did not create him to live for man's own sake or for man's selfish purpose. Man was created for somebody else — for woman. Yes, God made man for woman. Are you disappointed, men? Well, you should not be. Without woman, man leads himself into self-destruction.

Many of the ladies are smiling!

But don't worry, men. We won't lose anything, because God created woman not for woman's sake, but to serve man!

Women throughout the world have one thing in common. They always try to make themselves beautiful, putting on expensive makeup, arranging their hair, wearing beautiful dresses, and even doing beauty exercises. And for what? For themselves? No, for the delight of men!

Let's say a lady gets all dressed up and goes out to some social event. If only other women comment on her beautiful dress, she will soon be disturbed and think that something is wrong with her. What she is looking for is a compliment from a man. And if all the men there were just crazy about her dress, her hair, or her beauty, she would indeed feel that she was in heaven, on "cloud nine."

God gave us five senses and sense organs—eyes, ears, mouth, nose, and so on. And the purpose of all this is so that we can relate to an object, or someone else. Actually, these organs are not working for you, but for your object.

We have not realized this fundamental truth, that God created everything in this universe to be complementary. All things are made for other things.

Then what is the ideal couple, the ideal husband and wife? Well, after the wedding, the newly-wed bride and bridegroom go on their honeymoon. At first everything is usually most romantic. They confess their love to each other, saying, "I love you so much." They say, "I love you so very much. You are more than my life. I was born solely for you. Even unto my death, I love you!"

These are all most unselfish sentiments. But the problem comes when those pledges don't last more than three days!

However, if any married couple ever carried out those promises and truly loved each other unselfishly, then that would be the ideal couple—the ideal husband and wife in the sight of God. You know we are to live for each other. We are to exchange our lives. We are to fulfill each other's lives. This is the beauty and happiness of life. You by yourself can never fulfill your own life. The universe is not made that way.

What is the definition of a patriot? I know Americans respect and admire Abraham Lincoln. Why? He is respected because he is a patriot. A patriot is one who gives himself unselfishly for the benefit and well-being of the nation and for the welfare of his own countrymen. That is the true patriot. And Abraham Lincoln surely was such a man. He gave himself even to death for his country.

According to this same principle, who could we say is the greatest man in all history? Who is the Saint of all saints? There is one who surpasses all others. Jesus Christ. Yes, Jesus Christ was indeed the Saint of all saints, because he set the supreme example of a giving, loving, and unselfish way of life. And he is the one who said, "Love your enemy." He really lived that principle. He even gave his life for his enemies.

The Bible teaches this one principle from cover to cover, this selfless way of life in God. Jesus said there is no greater love than being able to lay down your life for your friend —or for your enemy.

From the very beginning, God has been constantly working to bring humanity into the knowledge of this selfless way of life. One day God will bring the perfection of that kind of life on this earth. That will be the day of the kingdom of God.

To this end, throughout history God has been using all good religions of the world as His tools, His instruments to bring mankind to the knowledge of God's selfless way of life. It is for this reason that all good religions have one teaching in common: selfless love, the selfless way of life. The essence of the teachings of good religions is love and sacrifice.

Then what is evil? What is unhappiness? What is sorrow? What is despair? Nobody wants these things. These are the products of the exact opposite of the way of God. In selfishness there is no peace. In hatred and selfishness there is no joy. In selfish greed there is neither harmony nor unity.

In the beginning, God created a world of goodness in which only His unselfish way of life would prevail. That was His ideal. However, the master of evil came into being and twisted the way of life around, from unselfish giving to selfish taking.

The first woman, Eve, was subjugated by the selfish love of Lucifer, the fallen angel. And Eve subjugated the first man, Adam, with a selfish motive, plunging all humanity into the darkness of selfishness and greed. *This reversal of God's principle was the beginning of evil.*

All evil came from selfishness. A world of greed and self-destruction was the result, and history has often been a nightmare. That characterizes the world in which we live today.

You might be thinking, "Rev. Moon, your ideas sound good, but I'm afraid you are too idealistic. How could a totally unselfish world be possible?"

Let's look at the practical side of it. Suppose there is someone who truly loves you, 100 percent unselfishly. Oh, you are a happy person! You are bubbling with joy because of the knowledge that someone loves you so much. You want to give something back to that person to show that you love him, too. Isn't that right?

Would you be stingy about returning that love, so that you discounted 40 or 50 percent of the amount of love you receive and kept that in your pocket, only returning 50 percent to him? Or would you like to out-love that person and try to give more love than he gives you? What is your reaction?

I know your answer. You want to give more. You want to out-love that person. It is human nature never to be stingy about love. So when there is someone who truly loves you, you always want to do more for that person. You want to make him happier. Do you agree with me? An unselfish deed always brings an unselfish reward. Isn't that so?

Your deeds of love will never be lost. When I love Mr. Pak with 100 percent unselfish love, then that love will not only reach its destination, but also bring back 100 percent love, plus interest.

Love forms a circular motion of give and take, and each time it brings back more love. It goes round and round, each time increasing the amount of love returned, creating endless motion. Circular motion alone can bring prosperity. In His wisdom, God set the principle of eternity in circular motion. Therefore, all of God's creation sustains its life in circular motion.

When there is an interaction of give and take of love in oneness, there is harmony and stimulation. The result will be joy, freedom, and prosperity. Each action of give and take returns the original investment plus interest coming with it. This is the way to become prosperous.

We commonly hear parents say to their children, "Be good. Be nice to others. Be a good man, and you will be blessed." This is very abstract advice. What does it mean?

What is the definition of a good man? Essentially, he is a selfless person, a God-like person. And one who lives in God's selfless way will never diminish but become prosperous in the sight of God.

The more you practice the way of life of God, the more you resemble God, the more you become God-like. When you live God's way of life, you will emerge as a leader in your own world. You will become the central figure, just as God is the central figure of the entire universe.

Let's say that in a household there are 10 members— two parents and eight children. Let's say the youngest son serves each of the other nine members of his family in the most loving, selfless way. Even though he is the youngest son, he will gain a central position in the family. He is earning more respect than anyone else, including the mother and father.

Why? Because that young son is truly practicing God's way of life. He is most nearly in God's position in his family, so he becomes the central figure.

So when you occupy the central position by love, by serving others, then in your own universe everyone seeks your influence. They will voluntarily come under your dominion. Actually, this is God's principle. It is only by serving, by unselfish giving, that one can truly dominate—not by power, not by force.

People do not like to be dominated. But this is because those who dominate usually do so for selfish purposes. Everyone actually wants to belong to somebody who loves him. Everybody seeks to belong to the source of love. This is human nature.

There is another important reason why we have to serve. What are the most precious things in your life? I said love and your ideal. Again, life is fulfilled when we find love and our ideal. But we cannot generate that love by ourselves. We cannot fulfill that ideal alone. We cannot have these by ourselves.

The essential value of love and the ideal which fulfills our lives comes from others, comes from the objects. We are in a position of receiving. Therefore, we must always be humble and meek, because we are in the receiving position. Our duty is to give our love unselfishly for others' sake, to fulfill their lives. We will then receive their love to fulfill our own lives.

This is the very core of the truth, the fundamental truth of God's way of life. Once we know this, it becomes our yardstick, the criterion by which we can judge and evaluate this world. With this principle we can tell where a person stands.

Besides this world of ours, there is another world we are to live in—the spirit world—which the Bible calls heaven. When we arrive there, we will see that heaven operates according to God's principle. We will see there the perfection of God's way of life.

Actually, this physical world is just our temporary home. We are visitors here on earth. Our eternal and true home is the spirit world. Therefore, while we are here on earth, we must recognize that this is our unique opportunity to prepare ourselves to be worthy of that heaven. We cannot be any better in heaven than what we have been on earth. How much we live God's way of life here on earth determines our place in the eternal heaven.

So once you begin to live according to God's way here on earth, you are already living in heaven. There are no boundaries between the life you live here on earth and the afterlife. This is why Jesus said that the kingdom of God is "in the midst of you." You can live in the kingdom of Heaven right now, right here!

Life for God is living for others, making one great circle of service. For example, I serve my family, my family serves the purpose of the society, and society is the servant to the nation. The nation is a servant to the world. The world, in turn, is to serve God. And God lives solely for you and me, for His children.

He is our Father, our True Parent. His sole concern is love. We must wake ourselves up and realize that God is our Father, and that His sole concern is to love us.

No one minds domination by unselfish love. No, we are all seeking to be dominated by love.

If America could make herself that kind of place where God's heavenly way of life could prevail, then America would truly dominate the earth in love. And the rest of the world would be only too happy to seek America's influence. We must create heaven right here in America and give that heaven to the rest of the world.

When we mention the Unification Church, with that big word, "unification," many people start to shake their heads. They say, "Unification? Well, so many people have tried. So many saints have tried. So many philosophers have tried. So many scientists have tried. So many military leaders have tried. But nobody has succeeded in bringing about oneness in the world, or establishing unity and harmony. Rev. Moon has a great idea, but it will not work. I feel sorry for him, because I know he will be disappointed."

To those people my answer is very simple. I tell them that I am not the one who will bring about unification. God is going to do that Himself! God created this world as one of unity and harmony. All we have to do is to restore it. Let's make God real in our hearts and start to live His way of life! Let God do His job of unifying the world. All you have to do is to let God come into your heart and use you as His instrument.

The question is not whether unity is possible. The question is whether we have God in our lives or not.

I am overwhelmed to see this wonderful, distinguished gathering here tonight. There are 1,700 honored guests. I asked my New York staff, "How did you accomplish this?"

I know what they have done! These young people went out to meet you with unselfish motivation. I feel sure that you came here as a result of the sincerity and earnestness of these young people—and above all, because of their self-less attitude.

The first time that one of our young missionaries approached you, perhaps you politely refused. When he came the second time, maybe you said, "No," with finality. When he came the third time, you must have said, "You are really sticky, aren't you? Go away."

Then the fourth time he came, you said, "Oh, I give up! These young people are impossible." By this time you began to see something in their faces—something earnest, something not quite of this world. Your heart was telling you, "I must respond to these young people." You would almost feel guilty not to respond to something so genuine, someone so unselfish.

I am sure that many of you came for that reason. Our Unification Church is here to proclaim God's love and His way of life. We do not want to become just an organization. We do not want to become an institution. We want to be a *movement* that will live God's way—not with our lips, but with our hearts and in our deeds.

In this day and age, God is looking for people who will *live* the truth. God is searching for serious-mindedness. God has been mistreated and abused throughout history. His name is spoken everywhere, but in vain. God is looking for single-minded fools—people He can trust, people who can do crazy things for Him.

The Unification Church was born for that purpose. I tell you that our young people are serious about God. We want to be fools for God. And we are such fools that we are willing to give up everything for Him.

Let me say one more thing in conclusion. You all have a Western cultural background. I have an Asian background. I have already become something of a controversial figure in Asia, and I am becoming controversial here in America.

There are people saying unkind things about me, things that are twisted and untrue. But one thing is certain. At least everybody is paying attention to what we are doing.

Now, the reason I come here is to serve — simply to serve. If I preach this way, and if I speak this way to the young people, and if we do not live these principles, then I am no good. Our movement is then no good at all.

But no matter how unkind people are to me, as long as we truly practice the way of life of God, then no other power can touch me or this movement and affect us even one iota. This is not any one man's movement, but God's movement.

I came here to love America. Is it a crime to love America? Of course not. Love does no harm. America belongs to those who love it most. So, in a way, I am in a competition for love. I want to love America more than any American does. That is my dream, my challenge.

Why? I love America because the Father in heaven loves America and the American people, and I love God as my Father. I love America as my own country. In Him we are one. In Him we are truly brothers and sisters.

I hope you now understand why I said at the beginning of my talk, "I love each one of you deeply and dearly." I said it, and I meant it—that in Him we are truly one people.

Yes, God created East and West as twins. Somebody has said, "Never the twain shall meet." But God created these twins of East and West to meet, to stimulate each other with different flavors, different characteristics, different cultures, so that we could have more joy and further enrich our lives. This is our purpose of meeting, and we must begin to fulfill it.

I believe that nothing happens by accident. It is no accident that we have come here tonight. We have a job to do according to the will of God.

Yes, this world has many problems. People are needed who can help solve those problems instead of being part of the problems. We are to be such people, working as the champions of God. We can attack the problems of this world only with God, by practicing His way of life. Then we can truly bring the Kingdom of Heaven on earth.

Since Jesus Christ shed his own blood for humanity, many great martyrs and saints have served humanity unselfishly, giving themselves totally. But today is an extraordinary time in God's schedule. Now God needs a committed champion of His own, more than at any other time in history.

We are here tonight to renew our determination to respond to the call of God, to pledge our lives and our resources, and to pledge to have America realize God's ideal here on earth. Let us commit our own skills, talents, and our very lives to this great purpose of God.

We are celebrating tonight, marking a new beginning for the challenge ahead of us—that is, to bring the kingdom of God into our midst. Our challenge is to all become true citizens of the kingdom of God. Our challenge is to make this New York, our beloved city, heaven. America herself can be heaven.

And when our life on this earth is completed, the record of how we lived will become the measure for how much heaven we deserve. This will be the standard:

—The love you unselfishly bestowed upon your fellow man;

—The service you willingly rendered for the benefit of others;

—The sacrifice you courageously offered for humanity and for God.

The sum total of these deeds will become your treasure for eternity.

These are the thoughts that I wanted to share with you tonight. May God bless each one of you, your homes, your work, and your great city of New York. And above all, may God bless America!

Thank you.

The New
Future of
Christianity

Madison Square Garden,
New York City
September 18, 1974

Ladies and gentlemen, I am very happy
to be here tonight. Thank you very much for coming. We
are gathered together in this impressive setting of Madison
Square Garden in the name of God.

My topic tonight is "The New Future of Christianity."
But before I begin this evening's message, I would like to
make one personal plea. I did not come here to repeat what
you already know. I have come to reveal something new.
I want to share with you a revelation from God.

There is only one God, one Christ, one Bible. Today,
however, in the Christian world alone there are more than
400 different denominations, all looking at the same Bible
from very different points of view with many different
interpretations.

What we are interested in is not the human interpretation of the Bible but how God interprets the Bible and what God's will really is. Therefore, no person by himself is capable of satisfying us. That information must come from God in the form of revelation.

And I want to share that revelation with you tonight. Since this message came from God, and since it is from God's point of view, the content naturally may be different from human understanding. Therefore, it may be very new to you. But what we need are new ideas — God's ideas — because man has exhausted all of his own ideas already. That is the reason for my coming to talk to you tonight. So I ask each one of you to open your mind and open your heart, so that the spirit of God can speak to you directly.

For 2,000 years, Christians of the world have been looking forward to one great culminating day as prophesied in the Bible — the day of the Second Coming of the Lord. Since this has been the promise of God, the Second Coming of Christ will definitely be fulfilled.

Why is the Lord coming a second time? He is coming to consummate the will of God. Then, what is the will of God? Do we know clearly what God's will is?

God is eternal, unchanging, and absolute. And He has one will, which is also eternal, unchanging, and absolute. In the beginning, God had a definite purpose for creating the universe and this world. That purpose was the reason for creation. And God began the creation of the universe and man to fulfill that purpose.

According to the Bible, after the first man and woman were created — Adam and Eve — God gave them a commandment. That commandment was:

Of the tree of the knowledge of good and evil you shall not eat, for in the day that you eat of it you shall die. (Gen. 2:17)

God asked them to obey His commandment. God was implying that by Adam and Eve's obedience to the law His purpose would be fulfilled. However, God made the consequence of disobedience very clear. He said, "The day that you eat of it you shall die." The fruit of disobedience was death.

However, Adam and Eve disobeyed God. The result was the fall of man. Spiritual death came to mankind, and the purpose of God was not realized. The fall of man means their deviation from the original state that God intended. Adam and Eve departed from the fulfillment of the purpose of their creation. They made a wrong choice, creating the opposite of what God originally intended.

After their disobedience, God had no choice but to expel this man and woman from the Garden of Eden. The Garden of Eden is a symbolic expression of the kingdom of God on earth. Adam and Eve no longer deserved citizenship in God's kingdom, so they were cast out into the ungodly realms, the living hell—which was their own creation.

If Adam and Eve had obeyed God, they would have brought the Kingdom of Heaven on earth. What would that kingdom be like? Adam and Eve were created sinless, with the potential for perfection. And they were to grow into perfection by obeying the law of God. While they were growing into fully perfected man and woman, their relationship was to be that of brother and sister. They were expected to set the true tradition of brotherhood and sisterhood.

What is perfection? Perfection is man's total union with God. A man is supposed to be the temple of God in which the spirit of God dwells. Such a man is divine, as God is divine; that man is holy, as God is holy.

Jesus was the first such perfect man. This perfection is the state that Jesus was speaking of when he said, "Believe me that I am in the Father and the Father in me" (John 14:11). When you become one with God, His divine power is yours, and you shall be perfect as God is perfect. Therefore, Jesus set as man's goal to be perfect as God is perfect when he said, "You, therefore, must be perfect, as your Heavenly Father is perfect" (Matt. 5:48).

God created one male and one female. Why? After their reaching the state of perfection, God wanted to bring them together into one heavenly couple through the blessing of heavenly matrimony. God intended to begin His kingdom with Adam and Eve as the first husband and wife.

If that had become a reality, then God's blessing to be fruitful and multiply would have been fulfilled. He would have given them the power to multiply children of God. And those children would have been sinless and perfect. What else could they be? Sin would never have been introduced into the human race. By having children, Adam and Eve would have become the God-centered True Father and Mother—the True Parents of mankind.

If Adam and Eve had formed this first God-centered family, from them would have come a God-centered tribe, a God-centered nation, and a God-centered world ruled by God alone. Then perfection would have reigned from the beginning to eternity.

Where did God create Adam and Eve? Up in the air, out in space? No, right here on earth. Therefore, the prospering of Adam's family should have brought the realization of God's ideal here on earth, and God would have become the center of mankind. This would have been nothing other than the kingdom of God on earth in which God would have dwelt with men and women.

If that had been accomplished in the beginning, there would be no great divisions of races and languages. We would all belong to the one race of Adam under the one tradition of Adam. And Adam's one language would be our universal tongue. And, indeed, the whole world would be one nation under God.

So, in God's plan, all men are supposed to be born into the kingdom of God on earth. We are to enjoy the heavenly life on earth. And then, when our physical earthly life is over, we are to be elevated into the kingdom of God in the spiritual heaven where we shall live for eternity. That was God's original plan.

There could be no Satan, no evil, and no hell in that world. Indeed, God did not create hell for His own children. No good father would construct a prison for his newborn child. Why would God need a hell for His children? Only heaven was God's original will. Because of sin, however, people lost their original value and became human trash. Hell is like a trash can. But it was necessary only after the fall of man.

Then let us further examine the state of the fallen people and the fallen world. We read in John that Jesus says, "You are of your father the devil" (John 8:44). By the fall, man was brought under the false fatherhood of Satan. Man changed fathers. We left our true father, God, and united with the false father, Satan. The first man and woman became the children of Satan. Under the false fatherhood of

Satan, Adam and Eve united unlawfully as a couple without God's blessing or permission. And when they multiplied children, they all came under the same false father. They were all born as the children of sin, not the children of God. Therefore, the multiplication of sinful children from one generation to another has brought about this fallen, sinful world.

Because God is not at the center, this is a world of sin, a world of mistrust, a world of crime, a world of war. And we, the nations and societies of this world, can destroy each other and feel no pain. This is the kingdom of hell on earth.

The master of this world, indeed, is not God, but Satan. This is why John 12:31 indicates that Satan is the ruler of this world. We know this universe was created by God. We know God created us. But God is no longer the master, because people changed masters. Man betrayed God and united with a false master, Satan. This Satan became the father of mankind.

The fall of man has brought great grief to the heart of our Heavenly Father. God lost everything when His people turned against Him. That is why we read in Genesis,

> The Lord was sorry that he had made man on the earth, and it grieved him to his heart. (Gen. 6:6)

God was grieved because the exact opposite of His will had become the reality. If God's intention had been fulfilled, He would have been joyful. If the consequences of the fall were the result of God's own plan, why should God be grieved to His heart? Why would He have been sorry that He had made us?

Almighty God is a God of love, a God of mercy. His heart is compassionate and grieved at the living death of His children. He knows no person is capable of breaking his chains and getting rid of sin by himself. He knows that only one power can bring people into salvation — God Himself. And God, in His mercy, is determined to save this world.

What is salvation? Salvation is simply restoration. What does a doctor do to save his patient? He restores the patient to normal health. That is a cure. What would you do to save a drowning person? You would save him by bringing him out of the water and restoring him to dry land. That is a rescue. By the same token, God's salvation of man is simply to restore man from an abnormal, deviated state to the original state of goodness.

So, salvation is equivalent to restoration. God is going to restore the kingdom of hell to the Kingdom of Heaven.

God made His determination clear in the Bible: "I have spoken, and I will bring it to pass; I have purposed, and I will do it" (Isaiah 46:11). God did not say He might do it. He said He will do it, showing His absolute determination to restore man and the world to the original design.

How? By the Messiah. To restore mankind, God sent His only son, Jesus Christ, into this world as the Savior—as the Messiah. Two thousand years ago, Jesus Christ came into our world as the author of life. He came to transform all sinful people into Christ-like people. He came to restore the Kingdom of Heaven on earth. Therefore, Jesus Christ proclaimed as his first gospel, "Repent, for the kingdom of heaven is at hand" (Matt. 4:17). With the coming of Jesus Christ, people were truly at the threshold of the Kingdom of Heaven.

However, before God could send His Son to restore the world, He had to prepare the way step by step, starting with one individual and expanding to a nation, in order to establish a foundation of faith upon which the Messiah could come.

After all, this world had been Satan's world. If the Messiah were to come to this earth without a prepared foundation, the satanic world would destroy him. So God worked diligently and carefully to establish one nation, one sovereignty over which He could have control. The nation of Israel was the result of that preparation for the Messiah.

God prepared the nation of Israel as the "landing site" for the Messiah. Upon Israel's foundation of faith, God could send His ultimate champion, the Messiah. Likewise, Christianity today is the parallel landing site of the Messiah for his Second Coming. And Christians are supposed to be forming a foundation of faith for the return of the Messiah in the final hour of fulfillment.

Today, as never before in our troubled world, the Messiah is our hope! The mission of the Messiah is restoration —to bring fallen, suffering humanity out of this world of evil and restore man into the original perfection and goodness of God. He is to destroy Satan's evil sovereignty over this world and establish God's sovereignty.

Jesus Christ came as the Messiah of 2,000 years ago for this purpose—to restore God's kingdom. Today we are waiting for the Second Coming of Christ. The purpose of that Second Coming is precisely the same—the restoration of God's original kingdom. That is the one purpose and one will of God.

We Christians are today's chosen people of God. Christians are Christ's co-workers. So we are in a position to prepare a foundation for the Lord, to welcome and accept him when he comes, to participate in his mission of destroying Satan from the face of the earth, and to bring all mankind to salvation.

But today, Christians are not sure about the will of God. We are more interested in our own personal salvation, our own heaven somewhere, and the guarantee of our own little niche "up there." But that is not the way God intended Christians to be.

God is looking for His champions among the Christians of the world today. And the work of God needs a sacrificial spirit. How many Christians are now saying, "Use me as a lamb on Your altar, and out of my sacrifice save this world"? God is seeking a self-denying spirit. God is searching for the bearers of the cross for the 20th century. And today's Christians are deaf to that call.

Instead, Christians today are crying out for "my heaven," "my salvation." What about God? What about the rest of the world? Will you be able to keep your small piece of heaven when the rest of the world is crumbling? No. If, on the other hand, the whole world were saved, would your own salvation not already be included?

Today, if the Christian churches persist in the same individual-centered way, the spirit of Christianity is bound to decline. Before we cry out for our salvation, let us cry out for the fulfillment of God's will. We must liberate God from His sorrow, His grief. When we have solved God's problem, man's problem will automatically be solved. Then Christian fire will truly burn for the sake of the broken heart of God, not for ourselves.

In their 2,000 years of history, Christians had great opportunity to bring the entire world to God. But Christians simply did not clearly know the will of God. They did not act when opportunity knocked.

That same opportunity is knocking once again. This time the opportunity has come to America. If today's American Christians recognize the will of God in the present day and act upon it, we can turn the world upside down and right side up and bring heaven down on earth. The hour of the Second Coming of Christ is at hand, yet we are missing the signs of the times.

Instead of continuing to ask and pray, "Thy kingdom come, Thy will be done, on earth as it is in heaven" (Matt. 6:10), we can act upon God's will now and make that heaven a reality right here in New York, because we have already arrived at God's scheduled hour of fulfillment.

Each one of us is part of the body of Christ, so when Christ comes we are the extensions of his living body. If each one of us is willing and ready to nail his body to the cross in order to have our world live, then we shall indeed turn this world into the Kingdom of Heaven. To live and die for God and Christ—this is the privilege of being a Christian!

Remember, God's will is to save the whole world—not just Christians, not just churches. There is a universally known verse in the Bible which we learned as children in Sunday school:

> For God so loved the world that he gave his only be-gotten Son, that whosoever believes in him should not perish but have eternal life. (John 3:16)

The emphasis there is on the word "world." God so loved the world—not just the church, not just the Christians, not just one particular people, but the whole world. For that reason—to save this world—the Messiah is sent.

If you asked our Lord the question, "Are you the savior of only the Christians?" he would answer, "No! I am the savior of all mankind." If you asked God, "Are You the God of the Christians?" God would say, "No! I am the God of the universe, the God of all creation, the God of all people."

Two thousand years ago, people were awaiting the coming of the Messiah but for very self-centered reasons. They thought that the Messiah was coming as a sort of military conqueror to avenge them and defeat the Roman Empire and to reward Israel with great glory and power in an earthly sense. And they simply missed the whole point.

On the contrary, the Messiah was coming to Israel to use the people as a tool or sacrifice to reach out to the rest of the world, to bring the entire world into God's salvation. God determined to restore the entire world and to bring all people into goodness and perfection. If God could not do that, He would be a defeated God. Defeated by whom? By Satan! Then God would not be God.

Imagine yourself in the position of God. When God looks upon the Christian world today, I do not think He is pleased. He foresees a great battle to be fought and won. God must have a confrontation with the formidable power of the enemy, the power of Satan, the power of sin. For that, God needs a modern-day David to confront this Goliath, Satan. Do you not hear God's cry, "Where is My David? Where are you, My David?" And God expects today's Christians to respond, "Yes, my Lord! I am Your David. Your will be done!"

But the Christians of this world seem to be in a deep sleep. And the handful who are awake are busy fighting among themselves. The time of harvest has come in this cosmic autumn, but God has no workers to send out to the fields.

Ever since the fall of man, God has been waging a divine war against the power of Satan. That war has not

127

ended. The final battle is yet to come. Christ is coming for the second time, as the commander in chief, to wage that final battle. And that hour has arrived. Yet, alas, no heavenly soldiers are ready. Christians are asleep.

So far, God has only been able to engage in "guerrilla warfare" against Satan, not total war. However, God has been preparing for one great day, a heavenly "D-Day"— like the D-Day of the Normandy landing—when God can launch an all-out offensive. That day is the day of the return of Christ. That D-Day of God is at hand! The Bible is the record of God's patient preparation leading mankind into that final battle. The fulfillment of the Bible is the coming of the Lord—the return of Christ for that D-Day.

* * *

What is the Bible, more precisely? The Bible has been a book of mystery. However, the Bible contains God's message to you and me.

The Bible does not use plain language, but is written in symbols and parables. Do you know why God has presented the Bible in symbols and parables? Why did He not speak the truth clearly?

God has had to deal with the world of evil. Throughout the ages, God has hand-picked His workers, or champions, out of this evil world. Abraham was such a champion. Noah was such a champion. And God's champions were always in the utter minority in the evil world. If God revealed His strategy too openly or plainly, the enemy would use that information against God's champions. Thus, the Bible was written as a coded message, so that only God's agents or champions could decipher it.

Let me make an analogy. To protect her security, America sends out many agents overseas to collect vital information concerning potential enemies. When the home headquarters is communicating with these agents overseas, particularly in enemy territory, would they communicate openly and plainly? No. No one would be that naive. They would communicate in coded messages — secret messages —so that the enemy could not decipher them.

Throughout history, righteous people have faced nothing but suffering on this earth simply because they were in enemy territory, and Satan did not want to have God's agents prosper. Whenever Satan's forces discovered God's representatives, they tried to destroy them. We must realize that God has had to give His instructions in coded messages. Thus, the Bible is written in symbols and parables. In a sense, the Bible is intended to be mysterious. Then how can we know the true meaning of those symbols and parables?

It is simple, in a way. If you are an agent dispatched by your headquarters, and you want to decipher a coded message, then you must either have a codebook or communicate directly with your home headquarters.

By the same token, the meaning of the symbols and parables in the Bible can only be clear when we communicate with our "home headquarters"—God. This is truly the only sure way we can know the ultimate meaning of the Bible.

Two thousand years ago, our Lord Jesus Christ brought the blueprint for the Kingdom of Heaven on earth. However, he could not speak plainly about his plan even to his own disciples. Jesus spoke in figures and parables. Why?

Jesus knew the adverse circumstances in which he had to work. There was political pressure from the Roman Empire. There was the ruling monarchy who opposed any change. And there was a strong religious system and tradition. These could all be directed against the building of the kingdom of God.

Jesus came to kindle the fire of revolution in people, which would in due course change the structure and the life of the entire nation. But he could not speak plainly of any of this even to his own disciples. Instead, he had to speak in figures and parables, saying, "He who has ears to hear, let him hear" (Luke 14:35).

If you attempt to interpret the Bible literally, word for word, letter for letter, without understanding the nature of the coded message of the Bible, you are liable to make a big mistake. Therefore, in this day, at this hour, what the Christian world needs is a revelation from God. God must reveal to us His plan; He must tell us His timetable and give us instructions as to what to do at this time. God indeed promised that by saying, in Amos,

> Surely the Lord God does nothing, without revealing his secret to his servants the prophets. (Amos 3:7)

Tonight I am standing here in Madison Square Garden not according to my own will, but in obedience to the divine will of God. God has called me as His instrument to reveal His message for His present-day dispensation, so that there may be a people prepared for the day of the Lord.

Tonight I am going to concentrate on the divine revelation concerning the coming of the Lord of the Second Advent—the vital issue of the Second Advent—the most important question of our time. And in order to understand this more clearly we must first know the circumstances of the coming of Jesus Christ 2,000 years ago.

There is one historical puzzle that has not been solved.

For 4,000 years before the coming of Jesus Christ, God had prepared the people for the Messiah, as I explained earlier. Through His prophets, God had forewarned the people to be ready for the Messiah. God was working to build up expectation, and there was indeed great messianic fervor in Israel. And at the appointed hour, God fulfilled His promise. The Son of God, Jesus Christ, came to his own people on time.

Then what happened? History is the witness. We did not know him. We rejected him, rebelled against him, and finally crucified him on the cross. Why?

The Christian churches say, "Well, the answer to that question is, simply, God sent Jesus Christ to die on the cross. The crucifixion was the predestined will of God from the beginning."

Then let me ask those Christians, "What will you do when Jesus Christ returns to you today?" All Christians undoubtedly will answer, "We will receive him! Welcome him! Unite with him! Follow him!" Let me further ask, "Will you crucify Christ when he appears?" Your answer must be, "No!"

If that is so, then what about the people of 2,000 years ago? If they had accepted Jesus — as you would today — would they still have had to crucify him? No! It was a mistake! It was in ignorance that we crucified Jesus Christ. It was God's will that His people accept the Messiah. But we crucified him instead. And then Christians "passed the buck" by saying that was the will of God. Ridiculous! This is not acceptable to our logic. Something must have gone terribly wrong. What was it?

The people did not know who Jesus of Nazareth was. They did not know him as the Son of God. If they had clearly known Jesus was the Messiah, the Son of God, they would not have crucified him. "He came to his own home, and his own people received him not" (John 1:11). And listen to the testimony of St. Paul: "None of the rulers of this age understood this; for if they had, they would not have crucified the Lord of glory" (I Cor. 2:8). If they had only known who he was, they would not have crucified the Lord of Glory. It was a mistake. It was ignorance and blindness that killed Jesus Christ!

Christians of the world have not realized the truth about what actually happened in Jesus' time. If God's only purpose in sending His Son was to have him nailed on the cross, then why would God spend the time to prepare the people in the first place? It would have been much easier for God to send His son among the disbelievers, or even among savages. They would have killed him more quickly, and salvation would have come faster.

Then the question is, why did the people not know who Jesus was? Believe it or not, the first reason why God's people did not recognize Jesus as the Messiah was because of the Old Testament. This may be surprising to you. But the people interpreted the Old Testament literally. They did not realize that the Bible was in code. They did not look for a codebook. Instead, they took the Bible literally, word for word, letter for letter. In other words, they became slaves to the letter of the Old Testament.

Let me give you the evidence. The book of Malachi in the Old Testament has a parallel purpose to that of the Book of Revelation in the New Testament. It clearly shows the timetable and the last-minute description of how the Messiah would come. In Malachi, you will find these words:

I will send you Elijah the prophet before the great and terrible day of the Lord comes. And he will turn the hearts of fathers to their children and the hearts of children to their fathers. (Mal. 4:5-6)

Who was Elijah? He was a great prophet of Israel who had lived approximately 900 years before Jesus Christ, and who had ascended into heaven in a chariot of fire in a whirlwind, according to the Old Testament. So people believed that Elijah would literally return from the blue sky in a chariot of fire and announce the Son of God. This is what people expected.

But did Elijah come? The problem was, Elijah did not return in the manner people expected. The people never heard anything about his returning miraculously. However, one day they did hear an extraordinary declaration. A young man from Nazareth, whose name was Jesus, was being proclaimed by his followers as the Messiah, the Son of God. That was indeed an incredible announcement.

And what was the people's immediate reaction? "Impossible!" they said. "How could Jesus of Nazareth be the Son of God? We have not heard anything about Elijah." No Elijah, no Messiah.

In order to accept Jesus Christ as the Son of God, they would have had to disregard their 4,000-year-old tradition and throw their Bible away. But no one was willing to do that.

People at that time truly misunderstood Jesus, the Son of God. They said to him, "It is not for a good work that we stone you but for blasphemy; because you, being a man, make yourself God" (John 10:33). And they picked up stones, ready to stone Jesus Christ, the Messiah.

Furthermore, when Jesus performed many mighty works and miracles, people did not honor Jesus. They said instead, "It is only by Beelzebul, the prince of demons, that this man casts out demons" (Matt. 12:24). What a tragedy! Jesus Christ, the Son of God, the Prince of Peace, was belittled and relegated to the position of prince of demons!

Pontius Pilate, the governor from Rome, did not want to crucify Jesus, because he could not find any fault in him. However, Jesus' own people were the ones who were shouting, "Let him be crucified! Let him be crucified!"

The people God had prepared to receive him wanted Jesus to be killed, and to have the criminal Barabbas released instead of him. Was that the will of God? No! Jesus Christ was the victim of the ignorance and blindness of his own people. And they misread the prophecy—they misread the Old Testament.

Imagine that Elijah had come in a supernatural manner, in a chariot of fire from the sky, as people expected. It would have created a great sensation. And imagine Elijah appearing in front of the multitudes and proclaiming, "This man, Jesus of Nazareth, is indeed the Son of God." Then I am sure everyone would have knelt down and worshipped Jesus right there. Then who would have dared to crucify him?

However, that sort of miracle was not the meaning of the prophecy.

Malachi's prophecy of the coming of Elijah was indeed an obstacle to Jesus' successful ministry. When Jesus' disciples went out all over Israel teaching the gospel and proclaiming Jesus as the Son of God, the people repudiated their words, saying, "If your master is the Son of God, where is Elijah? The book says Elijah must come first."

Jesus' disciples were not well prepared to answer this question. As a matter of fact, they were not learned in the Old Testament. After all, they were lowly fishermen of Galilee and tax collectors. So the embarrassed disciples one day decided to go to Jesus to ask for his help in this matter. An account appears in Matthew:

> And the disciples asked him, "Then why do the scribes say that first Elijah must come?" He replied, "Elijah does come, and he is to restore all things; but I tell you that Elijah has already come." ...Then the disciples understood that he was speaking to them of John the Baptist. (Matt. 17:10-13)

This was a real shock to the disciples. And then they understood, according to the Bible, that Jesus was speaking to them of John the Baptist.

Was John the Baptist Elijah? Yes, Jesus said so. But the people were never convinced. They said, "Outrageous!"

Let us imagine we can transpose these events to our time. John the Baptist of 2,000 years ago was a person of tremendous influence, enjoying great prestige all over Israel as a great man of God—just like Billy Graham of today, a great Christian leader. Let us say some unknown young man suddenly appeared and began proclaiming himself to the world as the Son of God. As a student of the Scriptures, you would ask him, "If you are the Son of God, where is the promised Elijah?" If this man said, "Do you not know that Billy Graham is Elijah?" what would be your reaction? You would undoubtedly say, "Impossible! How could Billy Graham be Elijah? He did not come out of the blue sky. We all know he came from North Carolina!"

135

You could not accept that, could you? Precisely this same kind of unbelief confronted our Lord Jesus Christ. People could not accept John the Baptist as Elijah, simply because he did not come from the sky. The people of 2,000 years ago were stubborn in their belief that the prophecy of Elijah's return must be fulfilled literally, that he must come from the sky. They were the victims of the letter of the Old Testament.

Yet Jesus Christ continued to preach with power and authority in spite of scornful public opinion. The people could not dismiss such a man lightly. They wanted to be sure of themselves. So they decided to ask John the Baptist himself and settle their questions once and for all. They asked John,

> "Who are you?" He confessed, he did not deny, but confessed, "I am not the Christ." And they asked him, "What then? Are you Elijah?" He said, "I am not." "Are you the prophet?" And he answered, "No." (John 1:19-21)

John the Baptist denied everything. He said, "I am not Elijah." He even denied the title of prophet. Everyone knew and recognized him as a prophet of God, but he said, "I'm no prophet." Why? He evaluated the situation and knew that Jesus Christ was treated by his own society as an outcast. Jesus seemed to be a loser, and John decided not to side with Jesus. He thought it would be much better to deny everything.

By doing so, John the Baptist pushed Jesus into a corner, making him seem a great imposter without defense. After John's denial, Jesus had no further recourse on this point.

Then why was Jesus crucified? First, he became the victim of literal interpretation of the Old Testament. Second,

Jesus was rejected and finally crucified because of the failure of the mission of John the Baptist. We can read in Matthew that John the Baptist, waiting in prison to be beheaded, sent two of his own disciples to Jesus to ask the following question: "Are you he who is to come, or shall we look for another?" (Matt. 11:3). Is this the question of a man who has faith in Jesus as the Son of God? John the Baptist had earlier testified to Jesus at the Jordan River, "I have seen and have born witness that this is the Son of God" (John 1:34). Yet this very same person, with the very same tongue, was now confronting Jesus by asking, "Are you really the Messiah, or shall we go and look for somebody else?" How disheartening that question must have been to Jesus! What a man of little faith John was!

The mission of John the Baptist was very important to the fulfillment of the mission of the Messiah. God sent John specifically, "...to make ready for the Lord a people prepared" (Luke 1:17). That was John's responsibility as the forerunner of Christ.

Jesus relied very much upon the success of the mission of John the Baptist. When this very John the Baptist sent his disciples to Jesus to ask him, "Are you really the Messiah?" it was more painful for Jesus than if John had stabbed him with a knife. Anger overwhelmed him. Jesus refused to answer yes or no to that impossible question. Instead Jesus said, "Blessed is he who takes no offense at me" (Matt. 11:6). This was Jesus' consolation to John when he saw that John was failing. Jesus was really saying, "Poor John, man of failure. You no longer have faith in me. You are taking offense at the Son of God. I am sorry for you, John."

And then Jesus spoke to the crowd in indignation about John, saying,

"What did you go out into the wilderness to behold? A reed shaken by the wind? Why then did you go out? To see a man clothed in soft raiment? Behold, those who wear soft raiment are in kings' houses. Why then did you go out? To see a prophet? Yes, I tell you, and more than a prophet. (Matt. 11:7-9)

John was more than a prophet, because he came to bear witness directly to Jesus Christ, the Son of God. He was born for this extraordinary mission. God entrusted that glorious responsibility to John. What an honor for a man to be called "more than a prophet" by Jesus! Yet John failed to live up to this honor. Therefore, Jesus said in Matthew,

Truly, I say to you, among those born of women there has risen no one greater than John the Baptist; yet he who is least in the kingdom of heaven is greater than he. (Matt. 11:11)

John had fallen to the point where even the least in the Kingdom of Heaven was greater than he. The meaning of Jesus' statement has remained mysterious. Christians have not understood its true significance because they have not realized that John the Baptist was a man who failed his mission. Tonight we know the true meaning.

John the Baptist was the greatest among those born of women because of his mission, which was to testify to the Son of God. All the prophets in the past had had the same mission. But the prophets who came before John had borne witness to the Messiah with a distance of time between them and the Lord. John was born as a contemporary of Jesus Christ, so he had the privilege to bear witness to the living Christ when he appeared in person. So far as his mission was

138

concerned, John the Baptist had the greatest, most glorious mission of all. Thus Jesus said he was the greatest among those born of women. However, in carrying out his mission, John was the very least; he was the most miserable failure of all. All the prophets who had lived before him were watching from the spirit world. They knew who Jesus Christ was. But John did not. He doubted. He became skeptical and finally blind to Jesus' identity. In the end, he failed to maintain his own testimony to the Son of God. He became a man of failure and, therefore, the least of all in the Kingdom of Heaven.

I will give you another indisputable proof of the failure of the mission of John the Baptist. The people said to John, "Rabbi, he [Jesus] who was with you beyond the Jordan, to whom you bore witness, here he is, baptizing, and all are going to him" (John 3:26). Then John answered, "He must increase but I must decrease" (John 3:30). Christians have interpreted this to mean that John was truly a humble man and a great prophet. They believe that he felt in all humility that Jesus must increase, while he himself had to decrease. On the contrary, this is proof of the arrogance of John the Baptist. If John had taken Jesus Christ seriously as the Son of God, he would have no choice but to become one with Jesus and follow him wholeheartedly, rain or shine. He would have risen or fallen together with Jesus, bound by the same destiny. This passage shows that John did not in fact follow Jesus. He took an independent course and deserted Jesus. He did not, indeed, take Jesus seriously.

John the Baptist was finally beheaded. He could have been a glorious martyr had he been beheaded for performing his ordained mission: witnessing and proclaiming to the world that Jesus Christ was the Son of God! But he was beheaded merely for becoming involved in the love scandal of King Herod's family. That affair was none of John's business. Attending the Son of God was his sole responsibility. But John deserted this divine mission and suffered a meaningless, even shameful death.

This truth must be told, however painful.

Therefore, Jesus said of John, "From the days of John the Baptist until now the kingdom of heaven has suffered violence, and men of violence take it by force" (Matt. 11:12). This means that because of the failure of the mission of John the Baptist, the kingdom heralded by Jesus Christ suffered and was left open for competition. When a champion of God fails in his mission, someone else must take up that mission and put forth great effort to accomplish it. Thus, men of violent faith—like Peter—took John's position by force of their own merit.

However, had John the Baptist been a man of great faith, what would have resulted? He would have indeed become the chief disciple of the Son of God, Jesus Christ. If Jesus had been king, John the Baptist would have been prime minister. That was the position that God ordained for John.

In that case, then, the 12 apostles, the 70 disciples, and the 120 people chosen by Jesus all would have come from the ranks of John's own followers. John would have served as a mediator to bring unity and harmony between the chosen people of Israel and the Son of God. Who would have dared to crucify Jesus under those circumstances? No one! The crucifixion would never have occurred.

I am sure that many people who read the Bible must have wondered about John, "If he was such a great man, why did he not become the chief disciple of the Son of God?"

Jesus himself indicated the mission that John the Baptist came to fulfill:

> For all the prophets and the law prophesied until John; and if you are willing to accept it, he is Elijah who is to come. (Matt. 11:13)

John the Baptist represented the consummation of the Old Testament, the Law and the Prophets. He was the prince of the old age. Jesus Christ came as the prince of the new age. Had he been supported by John the Baptist, he could have stood upon the firm foundation of the Old Testament Age. Then the new age could have blossomed in the fertile soil of the accomplishments of the old age. The Son of God could have established his glorious kingdom at once. And John the Baptist would have been the cornerstone of that kingdom.

Had John the Baptist followed Jesus, the distinguished leaders of that society would have been the first to accept Jesus Christ as the Son of God. Then who would have crucified the Lord of Glory?

When God sent His only Son to this world to establish His kingdom on earth, don't you think He wanted to be followed by the most able people of his age? Do you think that God wanted only the outcasts of society to follow Jesus? Not at all! The simple failure of John the Baptist broke the link between the Son of God and the people. And as a result, only fishermen, tax collectors, harlots and lepers followed Jesus Christ. This brought great grief to the heart of God.

If the Lord is returning to the world today, is it not most logical that all the leadership of Christianity—the bishops, the cardinals, the pope, and all the evangelists and great ministers of the world — should become the first group to welcome the Christ? If they followed the Lord and became his first disciples, the establishment of His kingdom would be infinitely easier.

You may say, "Reverend Moon, by what authority are you speaking? What makes you so sure?" I do have the authority to say these things. God showed me the truth. I met Jesus. Jesus himself showed me these truths. And I met John the Baptist, too, in the spirit world. He himself bore witness to the truth of this testimony. After these extraordinary spiritual experiences, when I returned to the reality of this world, the same Bible I had been reading took on a whole new meaning.

Even if you cannot accept these things as the truth now, you must at least suspend judgment. One day we will all know the truth. Eventually we are all going to die. Every one of us will end up in the spiritual heaven where truth is like the sunlight. No one can escape it there. On that day we shall all see the whole truth.

However, blessed is he who can be humble enough to accept the truth while he has the opportunity here on earth. Your knowledge of the truth and of God here on earth will determine your eternal life.

There is a third vital reason why Jesus was not accepted as the Messiah. Two thousand years ago, the people expected the Son of God to come on the clouds of heaven, according to the prophecy of Daniel:

> I saw in the night visions, and behold, with the clouds of heaven there came one like a son of man. (Dan. 7:13)

But Jesus Christ did not appear miraculously on the clouds of heaven. He was born of a woman—Mary—the wife of Joseph. The people said, "Well, how could this Jesus be the

Son of God? He is a mere man, just like you and me." This was another overwhelming reason why the people rejected Jesus.

Some might object that Daniel's prophecy was not intended for the first coming of Jesus Christ, but rather for the coming of the Lord of the Second Advent. But I say this is not the case, because Jesus testified that all the prophecies and the law given prior to John the Baptist were intended to be fulfilled in the time of Jesus Christ (Matt. 11:13).

So the prophecy of the coming of the Son of Man on the clouds of heaven was intended for the coming of Jesus Christ 2,000 years ago. In those days there was no New Testament, and the thought of the Second Coming of the Lord was not even in the mind of God.

This prophecy of Daniel posed much difficulty for the ministry of Jesus. For instance, we can see that the apostle John warns in the New Testament, "For many deceivers have gone out into the world, men who will not acknowledge the coming of Jesus Christ in the flesh; such a one is the deceiver and the antichrist" (II John 7). This is what John was saying 2,000 years ago about those who disbelieved in Jesus Christ, rejecting him simply because he was a man in the flesh. They did not accept Jesus but continued waiting for a supernatural appearance on the clouds. John condemned these people in the worst terms saying, "such a one is the antichrist."

These historical truths have remained hidden from the Christian world. Today, for the first time, all these circumstances of Jesus' ministry are being brought to light.

Yes, our Lord Jesus Christ came to fulfill the mission of bringing God's kingdom to earth. But we did not understand him. We committed the great crime of nailing him on the cross. It was a great tragedy. Then later we claimed that was the will of God. How ironic!

The conviction that Jesus came to die on the cross has become the very foundation of Christianity. But this mistaken belief has been piercing the heart of God again and again for the last 2,000 years. God's heart was broken when Adam rebelled against Him and again when His Son was nailed to the cross on the Mount of Calvary. We have sadly misunderstood both God and Christ.

Why, then, has this truth been revealed at this particular time? Because the time of the Second Coming of Christ is near. And God does not want Christians to commit the same mistake made at Jesus' time.

Only with the revelation of the clear truth from the Heavenly Father can all the Christian churches become one. Yes, truth makes us one. If we know the truth, that truth will liberate us from our mistaken beliefs and disunity. And the plain truth of God has now been revealed.

The crucifixion was not at all the original mission of the Son of God but represented an alteration of his intended course. It was a secondary mission. It was decided on the Mount of Transfiguration. An account of this appears in Luke.

> And behold, two men talked with him, Moses and Elijah, who appeared in glory and spoke of his departure [his crucifixion], which he was to accomplish at Jerusalem. (Luke 9:30-31)

When Peter, Jesus' chief disciple, was informed by Jesus that he would suffer in Jerusalem and was to be crucified, Peter violently protested, as we read in Matthew: "God forbid, Lord! This shall never happen to you" (Matt. 16:22).

Then Jesus lashed out at him saying, "Get behind me, Satan! You are a hindrance to me; for you are not on the side of God, but of men" (Matt. 16:23).

Christians often quote this particular passage as proof that Jesus came to die on the cross. Many explain, "Look what Jesus said. He said he came to die. So that is why he rebuked Peter and called him Satan, because Peter opposed Jesus' going to the cross."

But that interpretation misses one vital point. Jesus rebuked Peter after he knew that God had changed His plan and altered Jesus' mission. Since the people rejected Jesus, God knew that Jesus could not carry out his primary mission, the establishment of the kingdom on earth, which required the cooperation of the people.

At that late point in his ministry, God then asked Jesus to fulfill only the limited goal of spiritual salvation. Jesus therefore began preparing for this secondary goal. And poor Peter knew nothing about this change in the mission of Jesus Christ. Jesus called Peter "Satan" because Peter's seemingly comforting words had no relevance to the will of God at that point. Peter spoke from ignorance and blindness. But Jesus could not risk losing this secondary mission — for then his coming would have been completely in vain.

Let us consider what actually would have happened had Jesus been accepted by the people of Israel. Indeed, he would have become the king of Israel; he would have united his disciples with all of the descendants of Abraham, 12 tribes of Jacob, and all the Arab tribes as well. All of them would have become one family of the Son of God.

Jesus Christ would have set up a heavenly sovereignty centered upon the nation of Israel. The constitution of the kingdom of God would have been promulgated in his time,

An invincible nation would have been established, with the sovereignty of God spearheaded by the last Adam — Jesus Christ — as king. Even the Roman Empire would have been humbled before God's kingdom. This is the prediction of Isaiah:

> Of the increase of his government and of peace there will be no end, upon the throne of David, and over his kingdom, to establish it, and to uphold it with justice and with righteousness from this time forth and for evermore. The zeal of the Lord of hosts will do this. (Isaiah 9:7)

After Jesus' death, his disciples marched toward Rome barehanded, suffering and shedding their blood. And within 400 years, the Roman Empire collapsed before this weaponless army. Had Jesus Christ not been crucified, but personally commanded this holy army, the entire Roman Empire would have come under the sovereignty of God during Jesus' own lifetime. In those days, the great Roman Empire was the hub of the world. God's plan of salvation was to restore the whole world. Thus, God prepared Rome in a central role so that once the kingdom came to Rome, it could be spread easily to the whole world. Had Jesus been able to establish his kingdom in the Roman Empire, then through Rome's power and influence, people in every corner of the globe would have heard his gospel while he lived on earth.

Thus, in his lifetime Jesus would have established the Kingdom of Heaven on earth as a reality. The nation of Israel would have been the glorious center of his kingdom. Then there would be no divided Christianity as we have today — no Roman Catholicism, no Presbyterianism, no Methodism, no Church of Christ. None of these would be necessary. You no longer need a vehicle when you have reached your destination.

You and I would already be citizens of the Kingdom of Heaven. There would have been no bloody history of Christianity—no martyrs. And there would be no reason for the Second Coming. A doctor is unnecessary if there are no patients to cure.

The sad reality, however, is that Jesus Christ was met with rebellion. Without the obedience of Adam and Eve, God could not fulfill his ideal in the Garden of Eden. And without people's cooperation, Jesus Christ could not establish his kingdom on earth.

So Jesus focused on his secondary mission, spiritual salvation. Due to the sin and blindness of the people, God permitted His son to be a sacrifice. That was the significance of the crucifixion. God allowed Jesus to die on the cross as a ransom paid to Satan. In exchange, upon Jesus' resurrection, God could claim the people's souls, though redemption of the body was not possible.

Therefore, God's victory was not in the cross but in the resurrection. The resurrection brought the salvation Christianity offers.

At Jesus' crucifixion, Christianity was crucified as well. At the hour of the Lord's tribulation, no one remained faithful. Everyone betrayed Jesus. Even Peter denied Christ. But with the resurrection, Christianity revived as well. Then for 40 days, Jesus rejoined and cemented the shattered fragments of Christianity. That was the beginning of the Christianity of today.

Yes, our salvation does come from Jesus' victorious resurrection. This is the victory of Christ, and Satan's power can never influence it. But the body of Jesus Christ was given up as a sacrifice and a ransom. In giving up his body, Jesus also gave up the body of mankind. Our salvation is limited to spiritual redemption, because the redemption of the body remained unfulfilled 2,000 years ago. And our world still suffers under Satan's power. Sin rages and dominates this world through our bodies. Therefore, St. Paul shouted out in anguish,

> Wretched man that I am! Who will deliver me from this body of death? Thanks be to God through Jesus Christ our Lord! So then, I of myself serve the law of God with my mind, but with my flesh I serve the law of sin. (Rom. 7:24-25)

St. Paul was living in the grace of the Lord. Still he confessed that he could serve God only with his mind, and his flesh served the law of sin. His body yearned to be redeemed; he still anguished over sin. And so it is for us. By accepting Christ, we receive spiritual salvation. But our bodies serve the law of sin under Satan's domain—until Christ returns and liberates us from the bondage of sin. The Lord of the Second Advent alone can give total salvation: spiritual salvation and redemption of our bodies as well.

Christianity's power is limited to spiritual salvation. Unlike the nation of Israel, Christianity has no physical base, so God's dominion in Christianity is over only a spiritual kingdom. Therefore, our great hope is the Second Coming of the Messiah. This is the hope of America, the hope of the world. America—this unique Christian nation—must awaken now and ready herself for the day of his coming.

American Christianity stands in the spiritual position of Israel 2,000 years ago. America is destined to serve as the Messiah's landing site for the 20th century. God wants to reach out to all people and has chosen to reach out first to America and through her to the world. America's role parallels that of the Roman Empire 2,000 years ago. As Rome was the hub of the world then, America is the hub of the world in modern times. Jesus set his eyes on Rome. And when Christ returns, he will set his eyes on America.

*   *   *

In our ignorance, we Christians have missed the true spirit of Jesus' prayer in the Garden of Gethsemane. There he told his disciples:

> "My soul is very sorrowful, even to death; remain here and watch with me." And going a little farther he fell on his face and prayed, "My Father, if it be possible, let this cup pass from me; nevertheless, not as I will but as thou wilt." (Matt. 26:38-39)

He prayed this way not once, but three times. He was sorrowful even to death.

Many in the Christian world suppose Jesus prayed this way out of human weakness, shrinking from his mission of dying on the cross. Nothing can be further from the truth! Under Roman tyrants hundreds of thousands of Christians were martyred. They never said, "Please let this cup pass from me." Simon Peter, when he himself was about to be crucified, told his persecutors, "I am not worthy to die in the same manner as my Lord. Do me a favor! Crucify me upside down." Even he did not say, "Please let this cup pass from me." When Stephen, the first Christian martyr, was being stoned to death, he did not say, "Let this cup pass from me." Rather, he died peacefully, praying for his tormentors,

Such bravery is not limited to the Bible. Nathan Hale, a young officer captured in the American Revolutionary War, said as he was about to be hanged, "I only regret that I have but one life to give for my country." He did not say, "Please let this cup pass from me."

Do you suppose that the Messiah, the Son of God, was weaker than all these people — especially if you think he came for the sole purpose of dying on the cross for world salvation? No! Were that the case, he would be unqualified as a Messiah. We have not understood the Lord Jesus.

The prayer in the Garden of Gethsemane was not uttered out of any selfish concern or fear of death. Jesus Christ, our Lord, was ready to die a thousand times over if that were the only way to bring about the salvation of humanity.

Jesus' concern was for his mission. He grieved at the suffering of his Heavenly Father. He was in turmoil because he could foresee the terrible consequences of his crucifixion. Jesus knew well that his crucifixion was not God's ultimate will. He knew his death would postpone the realization of the Kingdom of Heaven another 2,000 years, and that in the meantime humanity would suffer terribly.

He knew that millions of future followers would have to suffer, shedding their blood and being martyred as he had been. He knew Israel would be forsaken and desolate. And most of all, he had longed to bring victory and glorious fulfillment to his Father's throne in heaven, not to return alone through the crucifixion. He had hoped for a triumphant homecoming.

So, in the Garden of Gethsemane, Jesus made his final desperate plea to God: "Even at this late hour, is there any possible way that I can remain on earth to fulfill my mission?"

If we are to become true followers of Christ, we must fathom the grief and anguish that Jesus Christ suffered.

Furthermore, had the crucifixion been the full will of God, then Judas—Jesus' betrayer—should be regarded as a hero and awarded a heavenly medal, because somebody had to hand the Son of God to the enemy to be crucified. Yet, Jesus said of Judas, "Woe to that man by whom the Son of Man is betrayed! It would have been better for that man if he had not been born" (Matt. 26:24).

And why should Jesus shout on the cross, "My God, my God, why hast thou forsaken me?" (Matt. 27:46)? If his crucifixion had been the will of God, Jesus should have been overjoyed. He would have shouted, "God, I am honored! Rejoice, Father, I am victorious!"

Christianity today has maintained the traditional view that Jesus came simply to die on the cross. This is how Christians have rationalized the murder of the Son of God!

Today, people cannot believe anything unless it is logical. God is truth, and truth is logical. There can be no perfection in ignorance.

Christian prayer alone could not lift Neil Armstrong to the moon. Scientific truth was necessary. I myself was once a student of science, and I know that God is also the God of science. God's message has to be scientific, logical, and convincing to men of the 20th century.

* * *

Let me come now to the apex of this evening's talk by discussing how the Second Coming of Christ will be fulfilled.

We read in the Gospels, "They will see the Son of man coming on the clouds of heaven with power and great glory"

(Matt. 24:30). And in Revelation we read: "Behold, he is coming with the clouds" (Rev. 1:7).

But on the other hand, St. Paul wrote, "The day of the Lord will come like a thief in the night" (I Thess. 5:2).

One prophecy depicts the Lord appearing with the clouds of heaven, and the other sneaking in like a thief in the night. These two prophecies appear to be in conflict. If he comes as a thief, he cannot at the same time appear on the clouds. Shall we just choose one prophecy and throw the other out?

The people of 2,000 years ago did not know the message of God was in symbols. In interpreting it literally, they made a grave mistake. And when we Christians read the New Testament, we must not make the same mistake. We must read the Bible in the spirit of God, and discover the true meaning of its symbols and parables.

Two thousand years ago, everyone expected Elijah to appear from the blue sky, but he did not come that way. Likewise, they expected the Messiah to come with the clouds of heaven, but he did not come that way either. Today, Christians await the Lord of the Second Advent's arrival on the clouds. But do you have any guarantee that such expectations will not be disappointed this time? Let us be humble and open-minded enough to accept both possibilities— his coming on the clouds of heaven and his coming as a thief at night. If you fix your mind only on the Lord's coming on the clouds, and it turns out that he comes as the Son of Man in the flesh, you will most likely commit the same crime as the people 2,000 years ago.

However, if you are humble and capable of accepting the Lord as the Son of Man in the flesh—which is the only way he could come as a thief—you win either way. You will be assured of meeting the Lord whichever way he comes. If you could miss the Lord at all, it would be only if he came as a thief. If he comes on the clouds, you have no worry. Every eye will see him then. The television networks will make sure of that!

But I must advise you that God will not send His Son literally with the clouds of heaven. If you are gazing up in the sky and waiting for the Second Coming of the Lord, you will be disappointed. He will come, once again, as a man in the flesh.

This is God's revelation. Let me testify to it by reading the significant prophecies of the Bible. In Luke we read,

> Being asked by the Pharisees when the kingdom of God was coming, he [Jesus] answered them, "The kingdom of God is not coming with signs to be observed." (Luke 17:20)

Everyone would see the clouds of heaven. But Jesus said we would not observe the kingdom's coming. Did the people see the coming of the Messiah 2,000 years ago? No, they did not, because he came as the Son of Man in the flesh.

Next, let us examine a most extraordinary statement of Jesus Christ. Most people ask, "Does the Bible really say that?" Look in Luke, where Jesus said,

> But first he [the Lord of the Second Advent] must suffer many things and be rejected by this generation. (Luke 17:25)

If the Lord is coming with the clouds of heaven, in power and great glory with the trumpets of angels, who could dare reject him or cause him suffering? Would you? These are Jesus' words: He will suffer and be rejected, because he is coming as the Son of Man in the flesh. At first, people will have a difficult time recognizing him as the Christ.

Christian churches and devout Christians are expecting the coming of the Lord on the clouds of heaven. They are all looking up, waiting for his appearance. But if that expectation does not come true, and the Lord appears unexpectedly as the Son of man in the flesh—as Jesus came to this world the first time—then what will happen?

At first people will reject him and cause him suffering. There will be no faith on earth. There will be no initial acceptance of Christ. Many Christians will pick up stones to throw at him. Many Christians will call him a blasphemer, a heretic, a man possessed by demons. Those were the very charges brought against Jesus 2,000 years ago.

In Luke we read,

> As it was in the days of Noah, so will it be in the days of the Son of man. They ate, they drank, they married, they were given in marriage, until the day when Noah entered the ark, and the flood came and destroyed them all. (Luke 17:26-27)

This is the description of the days of the Son of Man. And this will happen when the Lord comes as the Son of Man in the flesh. The coming of Jesus as a man will herald the Kingdom of Heaven. But nobody will heed him. In fact, people will laugh at him, ridicule him, and persecute him, and do all kinds of evil against him. And in the meantime, the world will continue in its usual way, in carnal business — eating, drinking, marrying — until the day the Lord is lifted up to the throne of judgment. When the world recognizes him as the Lord of Judgment, it will be too late! The ark will be closed. The judgment will already be at hand.

Now, I want you to consider another passage:

> I tell you, he will vindicate them speedily. Nevertheless, when the Son of man comes, will he find faith on earth? (Luke 18:8)

Jesus questioned whether there would be faith on earth when Christ returned. Why?

History may repeat itself. Two thousand years ago, tremendous faith existed. People prayed in the synagogues morning, noon, and night. They constantly read the Scriptures, writing them on their lapels, reciting them every day. They kept the Ten Commandments and all the laws. They brought their tithes to the temple. They fasted and fasted.

However, when the Son of God appeared, they failed to recognize him and condemned him to the cross. Did Jesus find any faith? In the sight of Jesus Christ, there was absolutely no faith on earth. So, when he returns as the Son of Man in the flesh, there also may be no faith on earth. Millions of Christians and thousands of churches may never see the Son of Man coming, because it will be in the flesh.

Now, finally, let us read Matthew:

> On that day many will say to me, "Lord, Lord, did we not prophesy in your name, and cast out demons in your name, and do many mighty works in your name?" And then will I declare to them, "I never knew you; depart from me, you evildoers." (Matt. 7:22-23)

What does this mean? Why should these devout Christians, who are calling on the name of the Lord, be condemned as evildoers? What wrong will they have done?

Throughout history many crimes and sins have been committed in the name of the Lord, in the name of God.

There is no better example of this than what happened in Jesus' time. The people who plotted to kill Jesus Christ — and finally succeeded in crucifying him on the cross — were the very people who had faithfully followed the word of God day and night. But when the Son of God came to them, they committed the worst crime in history. They killed God's only Son, and they did it in the name of the Lord!

By the same token, when Christ comes to us once again as a man in the flesh, how can we be sure that the Christians of today will not be the first ones to cast stones at the returned Christ? Today we have the same responsibility as the people of 2,000 years ago. No matter how great our works or our prayers, when God sends His Son, if we do not recognize him and unite with him, he will say to us, "Depart from me, you evildoers."

If it is ever true that history repeats itself, then the Christians of today could become the worst enemies of the returned Christ. They may attempt to crucify him once again in the name of the Lord. However, even though the initial rejection and persecution may be very severe, Christ is not returning to be crucified again. The Lord of the Second Advent will be victorious and will finally be elevated to the throne of judgment and shall judge the world as the Lord of Judgment. When he is lifted up to the throne, then every eye shall see him. It will be unmistakably clear to everyone who he is. And those who have previously accused and rejected him will wail and mourn because of the evil they have done to him. But it will be too late. The Lord will say to them, "I never knew you. Depart from me, you evildoers."

The Lord is coming. And he is coming as a man. Yet, he is also coming with the power and glory of God. And he will judge the world. Only the meek will be blessed. The arrogant will see the unquenchable fire.

Then what is the true meaning of the "clouds of heaven"? Let us note once again that the Bible is written in symbols. Jesus said, "I am the vine, you are the branches." This is, of course, a symbolic expression.

By the same token, the "clouds of heaven" has a spiritual meaning, not a physical one. For instance, we read in Revelation, "The waters that you saw, where the harlot is seated, are peoples and multitudes and nations and tongues" (Rev. 17:15). The Bible indicates that water is a symbol for the multitudes of fallen mankind.

What are clouds? They are vaporized water. Water is often impure, dirty, with many foreign elements in it, but when such water is evaporated into clouds, it leaves its impurities behind. Thus, those people who are vaporized and purified from among the waters of mankind are symbolically in the position of the clouds of heaven.

Jesus is coming among those prepared people, God's people. He is coming among the consecrated, reborn Christians—those who are purified, elevated, cleansed from sin. They will form the foundation of the kingdom of God when Jesus returns to earth. This is the true meaning of the clouds of heaven.

God actually intended His kingdom on earth to begin with the first Adam and Eve. If they had been truly obedient to God and achieved perfection, God would have united them in heavenly matrimony and established the first family on earth according to His will. This family would have become the cornerstone of the kingdom of God on earth, with Adam and Eve as the True Father and True Mother of all people. The Garden of Eden is the symbolic expression for that kingdom. And this world would have been the world of joy for God.

Although the first Adam and Eve failed, God's ideal remained the same. God determined to realize that original kingdom and fulfill the world of joy. And 4,000 years later in biblical history, God intended to restore that kingdom of God on earth through another perfected Adam. Jesus Christ was that perfected Adam.

St. Paul called Jesus the "last Adam," or the second Adam (I Cor. 15:45). He came as the perfected Adam 2,000 years ago in place of the first Adam who had failed.

The restoration of Adam alone could not bring a kingdom. There had to be a bride, a mother—another Eve. So God intended for this perfected Adam—Jesus Christ—to restore his bride, the perfected Eve. This would have been the restoration of the first family, lost since the Garden of Eden.

Because of the rebellion of the chosen people of Israel, however, this never happened. Nevertheless, God is determined to fulfill His will. Thus, He has promised the return of Christ.

Approximately 2,000 years have passed since Jesus Christ's death. And now, God is once again ready to send His son—in the capacity of the third Adam. Throughout history, God has always fulfilled His goal at His third attempt. It is true that the number three is the number of perfection. This time, God will definitely fulfill His age-old ideal by blessing the perfected Adam and Eve in heavenly matrimony, thus laying the foundation of the kingdom of God on earth.

This ultimate condition is prophesied in the Book of Revelation as the marriage supper of the Lamb. And the

Lord of the Second Advent is that Lamb, that perfect Adam. The Lord is coming as perfected Adam, and he will restore perfected Eve. Then they will be lifted up as the first True Parents of mankind. At last, God's joy will be complete.

Shortly before his crucifixion, Jesus said to Peter,

> I will give you the keys of the kingdom of heaven, and whatever you bind on earth shall be bound in heaven, and whatever you loose on earth shall be loosed in heaven. (Matt. 16:19)

The error was made here on earth. Sin was committed here on earth. So the error must be remedied and sin eradicated here on earth. Jesus asked us to pray, "Thy kingdom come, thy will be done, on earth as it is in heaven." Earth is the problem. That is why Christ must come back to this earth.

Many Christians believe that at the end of the world God will destroy everything. The sun will be darkened, the stars will fall, and the earth will be burned up. A mere handful of Christians will be lifted up in the air to spend the millennium with Christ. If God did that, then He would become a God of failure, His original will forever unfulfilled. He would be relinquishing this earth to Satan. Then Satan would actually become the victor and God the loser. This will never happen! God is almighty. He will not give up on this earth. It was meant to be, and it shall be, His kingdom. This New York shall be His kingdom, too.

You can be the citizens of the Kingdom of Heaven if you meet the coming Messiah. He is your hope, my hope, and the only hope of America and this world.

If we fail to see him, however, then Christianity will have no hope. Christianity will decline. Its spiritual fire will be extinguished. The churches will become the tombs of the old legacy. Our world then will be doomed.

Ladies and gentlemen, I have come here to Madison Square Garden tonight in obedience to God's command. The Bible says,

> And in the last days it shall be, God declares, that I will pour out my Spirit on all flesh, and your sons and daughters shall prophesy, and your young men shall see visions, and your old men shall dream dreams. (Acts 2:17)

We are living in such an extraordinary time, at the birth of a new age! Heaven is quite near. And if you earnestly call upon God, He will answer you.

You must urgently ask Him, "How can I know if Rev. Moon is telling the truth?" Do not let me or anyone else answer that question for you. Let God answer you directly.

So, go in peace, and please ask God earnestly, sincerely. Confront God in prayer. God will reveal the answer to you.

The new hope for mankind is the Messiah. And that "great and terrible day of the Lord" is at hand! It is up to you whether that day will be great or terrible. If you meet the Messiah, for you that day will be great. But if you fail to meet him, then for you that day will indeed be terrible.

God bless you. Thank you for your attentive listening. *Kamsa hamnida!* Thank you, and good evening.